DT
92
.S22
1989

THE SHIFTING SANDS OF HISTORY: INTERPRETATIONS OF PTOLEMAIC EGYPT

Publications of the Association of Ancient Historians 2

Alan E. Samuel

University of Toronto

WITHDRAWN FROM COLLECTION
Silverman Library – BCC

UNIVERSITY
PRESS OF
AMERICA

LANHAM • NEW YORK • LONDON

Copyright © 1989 by

University Press of America,® Inc.

4720 Boston Way
Lanham, MD 20706

3 Henrietta Street
London WC2E 8LU England

All rights reserved

Printed in the United States of America

British Cataloging in Publication Information Available

Co–published by arrangement with the
Association of Ancient Historians

Library of Congress Cataloging-in-Publication Data

Samuel, Alan Edouard.
The shifting sands of history : interpretations of Ptolemaic Egypt
/ Alan E. Samuel.
p.   cm.
(Publications of the Association of Ancient Historians ; 2)
Bibliography: p.
1. Ptolemaic dynasty, 305–30 B.C. 2. Egypt– –History– –332 B.C.–
30 B.C. I. Title. II. Series.
DT92.S22   1989   89–5440 CIP
932'.021– –dc19
ISBN 0–8191–7396–7 (alk. paper).
ISBN 0–8191–7397–5 (pbk. :alk. paper)

All University Press of America books are produced on acid-free paper.
The paper used in this publication meets the minimum requirements of American
National Standard for Information Sciences—Permanence of Paper for Printed Library
Materials, ANSI Z39.48–1984.   ∞

To my youngest daughter, Marion
and her dog, Zoë

ACKNOWLEDGEMENTS

The present volume is the second in the series *Publications of the Association of Ancient Historians.* The publications committee of the Association, Stanley M. Burstein of California State University, Los Angeles, John W. Eadie of Michigan State University and I, wish to express our thanks to Alan E. Samuel of the University of Toronto for contributing this essay on revisionist interpretations of Ptolemaic Egypt.

The manuscript was produced by the author on a Macintosh computer using Microsoft Word 1. The files were updated to Microsoft Word 3.01 for editing and formatting on a Macintosh II computer, from which camera-ready copy was set in New Baskerville on an Apple LaserWriter Plus printer.

My Penn State colleague, Paul B. Harvey, Jr., once again shared editorial and proof-reading tasks with me in the production of this series. Scott Camp of the Center for Computing Assistance in Liberal Arts at Penn State handled the computer files and set up the copy, and Dawn Detwiler of the University Press of America provided production assistance and advice during the preparation of this volume for publication.

Eugene N. Borza, President
Association of Ancient Historians

CONTENTS

PREFACE

My intention in this work is to delineate some significant aspects of Egypt under the Ptolemies, and I have taken advantage of the invitation to prepare it to offer my own views on how the evidence on some of these issues should be interpreted, as well as presenting current views. The study of the period after Alexander, in particular its manifestation in Ptolemaic Egypt, is in the midst of great change. After decades of general consensus and great advances in the investigations of social and economic phenomena which contributed to that consensus, some central themes in Ptolemaic history which have been heavily studied in past decades are just beginning to be given new interpretations. Because these areas are intrinsically of great interest, not only for the understanding of antiquity but for comprehending human interactions and human societies, I have chosen to focus on them in my treatment of Ptolemaic Egypt, and to deal with other aspects of society which have been heavily explored in the past—economy and religion—only as they impinge on my chosen themes of ethnic relations, administration and royal ideology. Many aspects of Ptolemaic society which have received great attention in the past and continue to do so in the present—I think of slavery, law, the position of women in the social structure, demography—are mentioned here only in passing or not at all, because I have not written this study as a survey of scholarship or a survey of knowledge. Both of those tasks have recently been done by the best minds in the field, and I therefore can concentrate on topics which are of particular interest to me and which, as views of them change, will greatly affect our understanding of Ptolemaic Egypt.

Furthermore, even though Egypt in this period is an exceptional society, and not a paradigm for the rest of the Mediterranean, I believe the study of Ptolemaic Egypt cannot be carried out or even understood without reference to conceptions about the wider world in the centuries after Alexander. I think it is desirable to consider the effects of modern experience on the treatment of that period, and an understanding of the study of Ptolemaic Egypt also calls for a survey of the directions of scholarship in its treatment of the period of the Diadochi, particularly the manner in which modern historians (and ancient evidence) deal with issues of administration, concepts of monarchy and the Greek city-states in the years when Alexander's generals were establishing themselves and their kingdoms.

There are good reasons to approach the subject in this manner. The appearance in the last decade of several important surveys of the period, Volume II of *Le monde grec et l'orient*, by Édouard Will, Claude Mossé and Paul Goukowsky, under the title *Le IVe siècle et l'époque hellénistique*, then Claire Préaux' *Monde hellénistique*, and most recently volume VII,1 of the second edition of *The Cambridge Ancient History* means that surveys of virtually everything of significance are conveniently available. Peter Green's large *Alexander to Actium: An Essay in the Historical Evolution of the Hellenistic Age*, will be the most up-to-date treatment of the period. The excellent classified bibliographies of Préaux and the *CAH* also make it unnecessary to provide an exhaustive bibliography here, and so I present at the end of this introduction only some of the more general and recent works which can serve both as introduction and bibliographical guides to the field. Accordingly, I have felt free, in the interest of brevity, to omit mention of many fundamental monographs and articles which are indispensable to anyone working in this field. The reader will find all of these in the bibliographies to the works I mention above, and many of them turn up in the notes and bibliographical apparatus of the books and articles I do cite. Those last are chosen for their particular relevance to a point or argument I make here, or because they provide some information of particular use for explorations in the directions which I point out, and in some cases because they have appeared after the publication of the bibliographies in the new major syntheses. For these latter I give full citations in the notes, and a few frequently cited works for which I use abbreviations in the text are listed below.

I also make no attempt to provide full documentation of ancient source materials. Again, that is provided by the works I mention above, as well as in the modern treatments I cite. I am not concerned to prove positions or to convince, and I therefore cite only enough to demonstrate that there is some validity to an approach or a suggestion I make. I hope, however, that I give enough citation of ancient and modern material both to make it clear why I think interpretations should change or are changing, and to provide a guide to the study of Ptolemaic Egypt which will show what that society can contribute to the understanding of antiquity.

I am grateful to Professor Eugene Borza, not only for his gracious invitation to follow Chester Starr in the development of the publication series of the Association of Ancient Historians, but for his continued editorial help and scholarly advice. Three other scholars generously read my manuscript and pointed the way to improvements. Naphtali Lewis responded with care to my request for comments, Stanley Burstein offered detailed suggestions of material to be considered at many points, while Richard Hazzard caught a number of slips in the text. The manuscript has been improved at many points due to the help of these four colleagues, and constraints of space (and my own perversity) have precluded the full exploitation of their comments.

ABBREVIATIONS AND BIBLIOGRAPHICAL SUPPLEMENT

Atti del XVII congresso internazionale di Papirologia (Naples, 1984).

BASP: Bulletin of the American Society of Papyrologists.

CAH² VII,1: *The Cambridge Ancient History*, 2nd ed., vol. VII, part 1, ed. F.W. Walbank, A.E. Astin, (Cambridge, 1984). Bibliography.

Egitto e Società Antica, Atti del convegno Torino 8/9 VI-23-24 XI (Milan, 1985).

Egypt and the Hellenistic World, Proceedings of the International Colloquium, Leuven - 24-26 May 1982, ed. E. Van't Dack, P. Van Dessel, W. Van Gucht, (Studia Hellenistica 27, Lovanii, 1983).

Fraser, *Ptolemaic Alexandria*: P.M. Fraser, *Ptolemaic Alexandria* (Oxford, 1972).

From Athens to Alexandria: A.E. Samuel, *From Athens to Alexandria: Hellenism and Social Goals in Ptolemaic Egypt* (Studia Hellenistica 26, Lovanii, 1983).

Green, Peter, *Alexander to Actium: An Essay in the Historical Evolution of the Hellenistic Age* (Berkeley, 1989).

JHS: Journal of Hellenic Studies.

Préaux, *Monde hellénistique*: C. Préaux, *Le monde hellénistique: La Grèce et l'Orient (323-146 av. J.-C.)*, 2 vols., (Paris, 1978). Bibliography.

OGIS: W. Dittenberger, *Orientis Graeci Inscriptiones Selectae* (Leipzig, 1903-1905).

Das ptolemäische Ägypten, Akten des internationalen Symposions 27-29 September 1976 in Berlin (Mainz, 1978).

SEG: Supplementum Epigraphicum Graecum (Leiden, 1923 ff.).

SEHHW: M.I. Rostovtzeff, *The Social and Economic History of the Hellenistic World*, 3 vols., (Oxford, 1941).

State and Temple Economy in The Ancient Near East, Proceedings of the International Conference organized by the Katholieke Universiteit Leuven from the 10th to the 14th of April 1978, ed. E. Lipinski, vol. II (Orientalia Lovanensia Analecta 5, Leuven, 1979).

E. Will, C. Mossé, P. Goukowsky, *Le monde grec et l'Orient*, vol. 2, *Le IVe siècle et l'époque hellénistique* (Paris, 1975). Bibliography.

I
MODERN VIEWS OF THE PERIOD AFTER ALEXANDER

One hundred and fifty years ago, Johann Gustav Droysen's ideas of *Hellenismus* were just becoming current in Europe. Quickly, the notion of a blending of eastern and western traditions creating a new culture became popular in a Europe which was still profiting enormously from its exploitation of the east and south, Asia and Africa. Droysen's *Hellenismus* yielded to a different term, one which gave its name to a new periodisation, Hellenistic, *Hellenistische, Hellénistique,* and the concepts attached to this term and the new period were similar to those which had emerged as part of the ideology of colonialism and imperialism: the carrying of the rationalism of advanced civilization to the more primitive; the spread of more progressive governmental forms; the gift of technology to those unfamiliar with it; the quickening of economic activity in areas long sluggish or dormant; the enjoyment and adaptation of the exotic art forms of the easterners by the west. Only in the area of religion were the ideas of the spread of oriental cults into Greek lands envisioned differently from the evangelism of Christianity to the benighted heathen.

By the end of the century the concepts of "Hellenistic" culture and civilization were being disseminated in all the languages of Europe, and scholars in North America, who had never conceived of themselves as imperialists, shared and adopted those notions as enthusiastically as their compatriots in the older academies of Europe. Perhaps American ideas of "manifest destiny" made the idea of the spread of Greek culture as welcome in the United States as Kipling's "white man's burden" made it understandable in Britain. Furthermore, the final triumph on the continent of Europe of the idea of the nation-state as humanity's highest political creation promoted the view that the more-or-less organized kingdoms of the Ptolemies, Seleucids, Antigonids and others marked a great advance over the Greek pattern of quarrelsome and self-destructive social organization based on small city-states. At the same time, these kingdoms seemed to be more amenable to analysis from the point of view of *Staatsrecht,* which Theodor Mommsen had so impressively

1

explored for Roman institutions. Even for Americans, the new monarchies in Egypt, Syria, Bactria and elsewhere were an advance over eastern absolutism, and for all the industrial cultures of Europe and the Americas, the clear advance of scientific knowledge in Alexandria and other capitals made royal power and patronage the more acceptable for its fruitfulness. The historical sense that an earlier century had made of Philip's triumph at Chaeronea the end of liberal classical culture shifted to credit Alexander's conquests with the start of something new.

At the same time as ideology encouraged academics to redefine ancient history and expand the focus of Greek civilization to a period hitherto neglected, archaeological investigation and the emergence of documents on stone and papyrus created not only new evidence, but sub-disciplines to promote and exploit it. As the study of history in general moved to take account of social and economic phenomena, the appearance of documents of private life from antiquity, wills, government orders, leases, loans, agreements of marriage and divorce and the many different kinds of private letters, accounts and memoranda meant that classicists could join their colleagues in other disciplines which disposed of so much quantitative data. And, particularly in papyrology, the eagerness to transcribe and interpret the handwritings flowing across torn and worm-eaten sheets of papyrus lead to an unprecedented cooperation among scholars in France, Italy, Belgium, Holland, Russia, Poland, Germany, Britain and the United States. The concerns of a discipline which Max Weber was founding as Sociology were at the heart of the investigations which were being carried on by papyrologists and epigraphers; the assumptions of economic historians were being adapted to antiquity. Although the analysis of Marx was not much in vogue among classicists—who were, in those days, mostly gentlemen—the fundamental assumption that economic interests strongly influenced political and military action came more and more to affect historical interpretation, and the new information from documents and the new ideas about history molded the whole approach to the study of the centuries after Alexander, a study which was, after all, only a couple of generations old at the time.

MODERN VIEWS OF THE PERIOD AFTER ALEXANDER

By the time World War I broke upon Europe, the first generation of synthetic treatments of the Hellenic dynasties of the East had already appeared. Students of the ancient world could read *L'histoire des Lagides* and *des Seleucides* in the pages of Bouché-Leclercq, could examine *The History of Egypt under the Ptolemaic Dynasty* with the irascible Mahaffy, could investigate *The House of Seleucus* with *Edwyn Bevan*, trace the *Geschichte der griechischen und makedonischen Staaten* with Benedict Niese, follow the life of *Antigonus Gonatas* with W.W. Tarn, examine the art and nature of *Il Regno di Pergamo* with G. Cardinali, or see the later development of the greatest fifth-century Greek city into *Hellenistic Athens* as Ferguson described it. By this time also, what historians knew of the individual dynasts or cities was appearing in the pages of general histories, Cavaignac's *Histoire de l'Antiquité*, Gercke-Norden's *Einleitung*, or de Sanctis' *Storia dei Romani*, and many others. All these works shared a focus on the spread of Hellenism into the old kingdoms of the eastern Mediterranean and eastward as far as Bactria. They saw as characteristic the foundations of cities of Greek type almost everywhere but Egypt, with these cities carrying the characteristic institutions of Greek culture. They pointed to the development of a common Hellenic culture which stretched west to east in the Mediterranean, a culture paralleled by the linguistic *koine* or "Common Greek" which was spoken and understood throughout the area. Historians interested in tracing the broad lines of significance investigated the impact of Hellenism on specific cultures, looking, for example, at the manner in which the Jews, or some of them, became Hellenized and thus created the atmosphere for turmoil in Palestine, or, in a completely different area, how Greek-like art in North-West India influenced the development of Buddhist iconography.

At the same time, the newly-appearing documentation of economic and social organization, in particular from Egypt, impressed most observers into describing the period as characterized by increasing wealth and a burgeoning middle class, by tight economic organization and by pervasive central governmental control of religion, of taxation, of civic administration and even of culture. Admittedly, this description applied better to Ptolemaic Egypt than it did to the more loosely-

3

organized Seleucid or Macedonian monarchies, but it could serve there to some extent, as it did also for Pergamum of the Attalids. Finally, while the common opinion saw a degeneration in the originality of Hellenic literature and culture during this period, the evidence of royal patronage and of the appearance of Greek literary texts throughout the countryside of Egypt led historians to a concept of a broadening of Hellenism and a wider readership and appreciation for Greek literature.

Many of these themes were more fully explored when the Great War was over, in the twenties and thirties of this century. These were the decades of the giants of papyrology, men like Wilcken, Hunt, Vitelli, Jouguet, and the historians and interpreters of texts who so influenced their contemporaries' concepts of what the period had meant in terms of the overall history of antiquity. In religion, Cumont's interest in the impact of eastern cults on Greek practice was a dominant theme, while in economic matters Rostovtzeff stood above all others in his knowledge and his authority for understanding the period as one of quickening activity and an approach to capitalistic progress. The number, variety and quality of special studies of different aspects of the economy, politics, law, administration, military organization, religion, literature, science, family life, commerce and agriculture to appear in the twenties and thirties are truly astounding, and even more so is the extent to which these studies are still the fundamental grounding of our knowledge. In papyrology, the rush of publication provided many important documents from the collections into which excavation and purchase were pouring new texts, and the practice of publishing texts of lesser importance along with those which made significant individual contributions to knowledge meant that quantitative analysis of certain aspects of society in Egypt became possible. I think in this connection of Heichelheim's price-range study, which, although admittedly not very sophisticated in its use of statistics, tried to assemble quantitative evidence to trace price advances and the relationships between goods and currency. However, the years which, sad to say, are now often called the period "between the wars" produced much more than the framework of data, information and technical scholarship on which modern students hang more refined notions of the development of these monarchical societies. The

4

effects of the Great War and its heroes combined with the stunning impact of depression and economic collapse to create an idea of the period which has dominated our concepts until very recently.

Many of us who were children during the nineteen forties remember a time when generals were heroes and soldiers admirable. Even some of the enemy commanders could be respected as part of a war which was exciting and had some of the elements of a game. It was the awakening of the years immediately following peace—the revelations of the death camps, the sour recollections of many returning veterans who shared college days with us, and then, finally, awareness of the doomsday quality of the weapons used at Hiroshima and Nagasaki, the sustained tensions of the fifties and nuclear testing, that turned so many people to doubt the sanity of war and to reject it as an instrument of policy, and convinced many that the military were no better, no more competent, and no more honest than any other batch of bureaucrats. All this was very different from the aftermath of World War I. As a generation, the Americans who returned from the trenches of France carried with them some remaining shreds of romantic notions about what they had done; Black Jack Pershing remained a hero, Sergeant York stayed in the minds of his countrymen as an ideal, while the American Legion burgeoned into an important political role to supplement cultural activities like beer, bingo and stags. North America was not alone in its respect for warlike military leadership. Throughout the commonwealth Earl Haig schools were named to commemorate the general who had done so much to assure that there would be few students in them. In Germany, Hindenberg was a name to be conjured with, and the French idealized their generals enough so that, twenty years later, many would follow old Petain into disgrace.

I think that the attitudes prevalent in the decades after World War I influenced both the popularity of the history of the period after Alexander, and the views taken of the men and events from 336 to 30 B.C. War (in a good cause) was justifiable, its victorious conduct admirable, and successful leaders tended to have their success in that arena read as success in others as well. Men like Ptolemy, Lysimachus, Seleucus, Antigonus, Demetrius were evaluated in terms of their ability to defeat their enemies

5

militarily and establish themselves with some permanence in territories through which Alexander had marched. Antigonus was eventually a failure, Demetrius always so, while Seleucus clearly had done better and Ptolemy best of all in parlaying generalship and satrapy into kingdom. Few asked why troops followed or cities welcomed the brilliance and charisma of Demetrius, who at the very least, offered the opposite of stability.

The same attitudes showed in the approaches to the heirs of the successors. Ptolemy II and III were sage kings who bent their efforts to the successful managing of a malleable and promising land, while at the same time were effective in military activities either by engaging in adventures which successful or, if not, faced little real threat in defeat. Bickerman's *Institutions des Séleucides* saw the structure of Seleucid government in terms of need for qualities like military competence and administrative organization. The history of the period was interpreted as a struggle for imperial supremacy, first among the dynasts who succeeded Alexander and then those who followed them in the third century B.C., later shifting to a resistance to Roman encroachment by Philip V, Antiochus III, and others. While I do not suggest that the clash of dynasts and Rome were comprehended as parallel to the clash of empires which culminated in the Great War, I believe that the comprehension of causes, motivations and purposes which influenced events after the death of Alexander was limited by the historical imagination inspired by the war of 1914-1918.

If there were limitations of imagination, there were also expansions, and these showed in the kinds of studies carried on in the years after 1918. The most notable of the expansions came with the weight given to economic and social considerations as part of history. It may be that the impact of Marxist thought and its political application as part of the Bolshevik revolution intensified attention to economic matters as determinative of politics. Certainly Rostovtzeff, no friend to the communist theorists, wrote his *Economic and Social History of the Hellenistic World* with the view that economic aspects of human activity were as historically significant—or more so—as political and military. That massive work capped two decades of intensive investigation of the economic activity of the dynasts of the third century and after. Rostovtzeff's own *A Large Estate in Egypt in the*

6

third century B.C., Schnebel's *Landwirtschaft im hellenistischen Aegypten*, Préaux' *L'Économie royale des Lagides*, are examples, for Egypt, of large studies to which the now-plentiful papyrological evidence could be turned. These, and a large number of smaller and more specialized studies were influenced by the acceptance of economic considerations as influential or determinative in the creation of institutions; as the Egyptian economy, like all ancient economies, was primarily agricultural, the institutions generated by the desire to maximise production would naturally relate primarily to the land, and so the Ptolemies developed a complex agricultural bureaucracy which was quite successful in controlling farming activity and generating revenue. The historians shared with John Maynard Keynes the idea that governments could play a role in determining the economic well-being of states, and like Keynes they tacitly assumed that, with economics so influential on politics, governments would want as much control as possible over the progress of the economy. There were more broadly based studies, like Mickwitz' influential "Economic Rationalism in Greco-Roman Agriculture" (*Economic History Review*, 1937), studies of slavery, banking, piracy, trade, monetary policy and metrology and many other areas, some of which extended to many parts of the Mediterranean world in the period, others limited to individual "kingdoms."

Beyond economics, social relations of all sorts were subjected to scrutiny, and the growing democratization of society in Europe and North America undoubtedly contributed to this. Slavery and legal institutions were explored intensively, and religion received a more sympathetic scrutiny than had been the case earlier. But again, as the society of the twenties and thirties made academics more familiar with and accepting of governmental involvement in private life, scholars interpreted their evidence in accordance with their understanding that deliberate government policy and planning often lay behind social institutions and activities. Thus, for example, the growth of cults like that of Isis and Sarapis were seen as part of Ptolemaic political policy, and the omnipresent dynastic cults of the period were given entirely political explanation. Furthermore, the increasing awareness of the effects on society of the imperialism of the nineteenth century prompted a sensitivity to the

7

interactions between the governing Greeks and the teeming masses who populated the countryside of Palestine, Syria, Mesopotamia and Egypt. Scholars tended to make distinctions along cultural, not ethnic lines, rendering what was seen as a favorable judgment on the "racial" policies of the kings. In Egypt, for example, language was understood as the avenue to power, along which Hellenized Egyptians could leave the lower classes and join the ranks of the dominant society so long as they were able to function in the language of the rulers. With a process like that in mind, it was easy to understand the interchange of cultures which had been made the hallmark of the period.

Many of these attitudes persisted or became even more deep seated after the Second World War, particularly insofar as social structures became—for a while at least—somewhat more egalitarian in the western industrial nations, and government, economic activity and social institutions were more and more integrated. There were, of course, also the holdover attitudes of earlier times; generations do not pass away uniformly, their members cooperatively dying in congruence with the great events which create changes in ideas. Tarn's attitudes toward Alexander the Great, for example, were still there to be dealt with in his publication of 1948. In general, however, judgments of the postwar period tended to be less and less charitable toward the intentions or abilities of the rulers of antiquity. Even the great Alexander has recently been seen as sacrificing a whole generation of Macedonians to his ambition, dealing his people a blow from which they never recovered. Eventually this decline in esteem would drop to the level of Sir Eric Turner's judgment in the 2nd edition of Vol. VII of *The Cambridge Ancient History* on the policies of Ptolemy II and the effects they had on Egyptian economics and society. What an earlier generation had seen as a planned economy which brought the brilliant originality of Greeks to promote prosperity and expansion, Turner reinterpreted to reveal progressively increasing exploitation and pressure on the population which brought about a "bankruptcy" of Egypt and produced a great deal of internal turmoil, and lay at the door of "competitive dynastic wars" responsibility for the need to squeeze all available resources out of the country. The argument is as persuasive to readers of the nineteen-eighties as were Rostovtzeff's and Préaux' approving assesments to scholars of the thirties and forties. But one is entitled to wonder whether we middle-class academics of the seventies and eighties, feeling the constraints of a poorer economic climate and less friendly governments, might have been pushed by experience to view the same evidence a little differently, just as we have come to regard war as a non-productive expense of government which puts serious pressures on much of the population.

There has also been a major change in our assessment of the phenomenon of the period which had long been seen as its greatest characteristic, what has been called syncretism. The jurists, at least, never had to contend with the concept, for it was clear that among Greeks, Hellenic concepts and rules of jurisprudence applied, while "native" law remained vital to serve the needs of the non-hellenized. This was clearest in Egypt, where papyrus texts gave explicit documentation for the separate administration of the two types of law. Indeed, this "co-existence" in legal affairs was seen as part of the evidence for a Greek and Macedonian administration which was not racially discriminatory. In the last decade, however, that "co-existence" has been discerned in many aspects of life beside the legal. In Egypt, where evidence is plentiful, we now understand that native culture and literature flourished alongside the Greek, and that the two had very little influence over each other. In religious practice, natives continued a close association with Egyptian temples and practices and few involved themselves in Greek religion, while Greeks were rarely to be found in any involvement in traditional Egyptian religion. While it was not, apparently, difficult for a "hellenized" Egyptian to operate freely in the Greek milieu, that hellenization meant a wholesale adoption of Greek culture, not merely facility in language, for we find very little evidence of people with their feet in both worlds, so to speak. And decolonization in the modern world has prompted Édouard Will to reflect on the colonial nature of the dominance of Hellenism in the areas controlled by the Macedonian monarchies. In the broader scope of the whole Mediterreanean, the spreading cults which had formerly been regarded as "orientalized" have come to be seen more as hellenized cults of oriental deities, quite a different matter, and analogous to an old Greek tradition of accepting eastern gods and

9

goddesses into religious observation. The new view of the separation between Greek and native societies at this time was propounded most fully and in its most general application in 1978 by Claire Préaux in *Le monde hellénistique;* it may be no accident that a reinterpretation of the evidence to argue against adaptation and for the continuing existence of two separate cultures came from a Belgian scholar writing at a time when that country was experiencing a strong revival of Flemish cultural nationalism and attempting to provide for the survival of the Flamands in the hitherto dominant French-speaking milieu. And it may also be no accident that my own perceptions of cultural co-existence may have been strongly influenced by my experience of two decades of resurgent Francophones in Canada.

Recent work shows that the consensus which gave the period after Alexander coherence and meaning for the flow of history in antiquity has thoroughly broken up. No longer can we assert confidently that the world which Alexander opened to the Greeks provided an opportunity for Hellenism to blend with many local cultures to create a new and universal culture for the Mediterranean. The idea that the amalgamation of religious ideas fertilized the ground to make people ready for the Christian message, a notion which could be adopted happily by evangelical Christians and rationalist atheists alike, no longer seems to have so much validity. In other areas, the evidence now suggests a greater diversity of culture and cultures among the peoples of the Mediterranean, a diversity which can be understood as leading into the multicultural community which was the Roman Empire. The survival of the many languages, religious traditions, cultural communities and even political separatism which seems to have continued despite the Augustan unification of the Mediterranean has attracted attention in recent years, again, perhaps due to a greater toleration of genuine diversity in the modern world. In the same way, writers about the period before Rome gained political supremacy have been willing to approach different areas without attempting to fit them into a unified picture of the history of the period.

This does mean, however, that knowledge of the period in light of most recent writing seems fragmented; the establishment of an Isis cult center in Spain or on the Balearics is not necessarily seen as the same phenomenon which brought it to Athens or Cyrene; the dynastic cult of the Seleucids may not have been organized along Ptolemaic lines, or even have served the same social purposes it fulfilled in Egypt; even monarchy as an institution may have varied strikingly from place to place and time to time; we cannot presume from Egyptian parallels the development of Judaism in Palestine, or vice-versa. All these are examples of the kinds of issues with which scholars have struggled, and all the caveats are now observed. An illustration of the result, as I have remarked in my review of CAH^2 VII,1 (*Phoenix*, 40, 1986), is a change from the coherence and consensus aspect of the first edition of the volume of the *Cambridge Ancient History* which dealt with the period, to a second-edition volume with little internal cohesion and great diversity, not only in appraisals of the period and in the manner of looking at it, but even in the estimate of what is worth discussion.

Interestingly enough, this state of affairs does not seem to distress contemporary historians. I suppose we are all accustomed to a world in which influential forces seem to work at cross purposes. An ancient experience affected by chance as much as or more than cooperation, in which governments may do similar things for very different purposes, or try to achieve similar results by strikingly different means, merely seems to us the norm of life. More and more we disbelieve the experts, and consider that decisions are made in ignorance, deception, stupidity or by accident, and we are content to accept the same situation in antiquity as we live with in the present.

I do not suggest that the lines of research today are strikingly different from what they have been for most of the century. Even the increasing numbers of female scholars and greater attention to the situation of women have not radically affected the subjects studied or the general pattern of investigation—yet. The papyrologists and epigraphers continue to edit and interpret texts. Chronology remains a major concern. Religious matters are still the subject of a great deal of discussion. Each of the areas around the Mediterranean receives its share of special studies, and various aspects of policy, administration and even ideology of individual monarchs come in for attention. But less and less is the Mediterranean world in this period seen as a unit, and still

11

less has there developed a new interpretation of the significance of the period for human history, to replace the old view that it was a transition from and transformation of Hellenism by which early traditions received new directions from eastern influences, and went on to create the new world of Christian Rome.

II

THE SUCCESSORS OF ALEXANDER

The major political events in the decades after Alexander's death are well known. Not only from Diodorus' history, extant down to the Battle of Issus in 301, but in other sources, biographical like Plutarch, annalistic like Porphyry, we can put together a narrative account of events, often very detailed,[1] which shows the manner in which the generals interacted and fought to establish themselves in the regions won by their erstwhile leader. Modern historians have no trouble understanding the conflict which arose almost immediately, which moved through the machinations of Perdiccas' failed attempt to maintain the unity of the empire under his own leadership, through the conflicts of the successor generals, their attempts at agreement, first at Triparadeisus settling the basic divisions of the realm in 321, repeated in 311, emphasized by the adoption of royal titles in 306 - 305, and settled with Antigonus' death in the Battle of Ipsus in 301.

The account of this period, in whatever length it is told, becomes for the most part a narrative of political machinations and military competition, with recent comment, perhaps due to changing views of military heroes, on the manner in which the manpower losses of Alexander's campaign affected the subsequent history of Macedonia.[2] Although many of the successors, Antigonus, Seleucus, Ptolemy and Lysimachus at least, were attempting to establish some stable form of administration and government over the territories they controlled, in addition to trying to protect or extend their domains and meet the challenges of one another, the ancient literary sources tell us practically nothing about how these problems were handled, and there are not many documents from the earlier period to fill in the gap. In Egypt, where papyri are plentiful in the generation

---

[1]See, for example, R.M. Errington's very close examination of the sources for and the period between the conqueror's death and the conference at Triparadeisus, "From Babylon to Triparadeisus, 323-320 B.C.," *JHS* 90 (1970), pp. 49-77.

[2]W.L. Adams, "Antipater and Cassander: Generalship on Restricted Resources in the Fourth Century," *Ancient World* 10 (1984), pp. 79-99; A.B. Bosworth, "Alexander the Great and the Decline of Macedon," *JHS* 105 (1986), pp. 1-12.

after Ptolemy I, there are practically no Greek papyri for the first reign. We see just a little of a chancery, influencing Egyptian scribes to date documents by a reign beginning in the year 305/4, while Greek scribes at the end of the reign dated as if it had started on the death of Alexander the Great.

The documents do give us a few hints about the manner of administration. One of the Alexander-priests named in the documents, P. Elephantine 2 and P. Hibeh 84(a), both of the 40th year, is Menelaos son of Lagos, Ptolemy's brother. The king used him not only in honorific positions, but for serious work as well, for Menelaos governed Cyprus after the death of Nikokreon in 310, and probably in the capacity of king. Bagnall's argument that Diodorus' designation of Nikokreon and Menelaos is non-technical and refers to activity rather than office is probably correct,[3] and would fit with other evidence of Ptolemy's scanty bureaucratic service. Ptolemy also had a *phrourarchos* on Cyprus at the end of the fourth century,[4] but this again is a military command rather than civilian administration. The shakiness of the administrative service is well illustrated by the difficulties Ptolemy encountered in Cyrene, with his agent-in-charge Ophellas behaving with a good deal of independence, with revolts there, and then, after Ipsus, using a family member, his stepson Magas. The major document illustrating Ptolemy's activity in Cyrene, the "Constitution of Cyrene,"[5] makes it quite clear that at the early state of Ptolemy's establishing control over the area, there were no Ptolemaic officials and no indication of any bureaucratic or administrative structure answerable to Ptolemy.

[3]R.S. Bagnall, *The Administration of the Ptolemaic Possessions Outside Egypt* (Leiden, 1976), pp. 40-42.
[4]*OGIS* 20.
[5]*SEG* IX, 7. The text provides for a Ptolemaic garrison and appeal to Ptolemy for a three-year period, while Ptolemy himself is permanently one of the six-member board of *strategoi* and makes the initial appointment of the 101 elders, but the relationship between the satrap and this very nearby city is not significantly different from the kinds of arrangments which the successors made with Greek cities elsewhere. Cf. also the comments on the text by P.M. Fraser, *Berytus* 12 (1958), pp. 120-127.

THE SUCCESSORS OF ALEXANDER

For the most part, all we have of Ptolemy's administration is military, figures like the admiral Callicrates,[6] Seleucus himself when he commanded the fleet and served at Gaza in 312, nesiarchs and other military commanders of lesser importance. The indefiniteness of administration at the time is illustrated by the career of the king of Sidon, Philocles, who held an extraordinary command but whose title is in fact unknown.[7] There are a few civilians of whom we learn, like the names of the ambassadors to Sinope sent to obtain the statue of Sarapis, the Aristoboulos who undertook a diplomatic mission to Antigonus in 311, Theodorus, the Cyrenaic philosopher mentioned as an ambassador to Lysimachus,[8] or some notables in the cultural field—Demetrius of Phalerum and the philosopher Straton, for example—but there is nothing administrative about this. Even the accomplishments and acts recorded by the Satrap Stele are military or religious, and the praises applied to the satrap are reminiscent of the expressions of praise customary for Egyptian monarchs. In the non-political sphere, that of the Alexandrian museum and library for which Ptolemy is so famous, we have surprisingly little evidence as well. Noted figures like Zenodotus, librarian from about 290 to 275 are known, of course, and we have reference to a figure like the Aetolian Alexander, grammarian and poet, who supervised the department of tragic poetry in the library from about 285 on, but the manner in which the institution was run is virtually unknown. We fall back on generalities, like the observation of the great encouragement of culture for which Ptolemy was responsible. True as the generality might be, we do not know how the king did it.[9] All in all, if we were forced to limit our statements to what the evidence actually

---

[6]Who has been studied in detail, by H. Hauben, *Callicrates of Samos: A Contribution to the Study of the Ptolemaic Admiralty* (Studia Hellenistica 18, Lovanii, 1970).

[7]H. Hauben, "Philocles King of the Sidonians and General of the Ptolemies," *Studia Phoenicia* V, *Phoenicia and the East Mediterranean in the First Millennium B.C.* (Leuven, 1987), pp. 413-427.

[8]Diogenes Laertius II.102-3.

[9]Virtually all of the detail about the mouseion and library in pp. 305-335 of Fraser's *Ptolemaic Alexandria* I relates to Philadelphus' reign and later, apart from the mention of a few cultural figures like Demetrius of Phalerum, Philistias and Straton associated with Soter, and Fraser emphasizes how little we know of the functioning of either institution.

tells us, we would describe government under Ptolemy I as informal, with little administrative structure, staffed by some Macedonians and Greeks but dependent also on relatives and friends of the ruler.

We are no better off for adminstration under Antigonus and Seleucus. Of Antigonus' finances, the organization of his realm and of his officers we have a few hints, as also for his "philoi," the nature of his monarchy and the royal cults dedicated to him, but extensive discussion begins with his city-foundations and his relations with the Greek cities in the territories he controlled.[10] Such scribal bureaucracy as there was under Seleucus showed the same interest in dating procedure as existed in Egypt.[11] As in Egypt, two systems co-existed, and the Babylonian persisted into astronomical records, which can only be understood in these terms. The confusion suggests a chancery which did not succeed in unifying scribal practice. And the texts of inscriptions which record the dealings of the successors with one another and with the Greek cities do not suggest the existence of much administration at all, with letters addressed directly from the kings,[12] treating matters which seem to have been handled directly by the king, and without reference to any officials in the kings' service, save for essentially military commanders from time to time.

Even the modern studies of the successors, for the most part, concentrate on the political, military or chronological aspects of the period, even though it was in those times that some of the fundamental lines were laid down along which society, the economy and culture developed for the next two centuries. The political nature of "successor" history is apparent in an excellent recent monograph on the period,[13] and a survey of scholarship

[10]Claude Wehrli, *Antigone et Démétrios* (Geneva, 1968), pp. 79-129.

[11]The scribes began dating documents and established an era with an epoch that began with the Babylonian year starting in 311, but later also used an epoch beginning with an accession year starting in 312.

[12]For the texts, C.B. Welles, *Royal Correspondence in the Hellenistic Period* (New Haven, 1934).

[13]Hermann Bengtson, *Die Diadochen, Die Nachfolger Alexanders des Grossen* (Munich, 1987), in nearly 200 pages devotes about 35 to non-political matters, and this is mostly cultural, art and religion, with nothing treated of administration or economic matters.

done in 1983 finds material on economic matters to fill no more than two pages, and most of that general and dealing with the period after the first successors, while in its catalogue of "Central Problems," economic or administrative issues do not appear alongside monarchical and political theory or religious matters.[14] This characteristic of investigation shows in the focus of most of the special studies which have become basic to our understanding of the period, works like Hermann Bengtson's *Die Strategie in der Hellenistichen Zeit*,[15] and Édouard Will's *Histoire Politique du monde hellénistique*, of which the first volume, carrying its account of events down through the first three quarters of the third century, appeared in 1966.[16] Often the focus on this aspect of history brought together as if unchanging the political and social institutions of most of the eastern regions through three centuries, as if the situation remained more or less static once the structures of monarchy had been set up in 306-305.[17] For the most part,[18] however, special studies which range beyond the treatment of political events and conflict among the immediate successors deal with the institutions of the various realms once they had become established and were settled down under later monarchs. The only recent study of Seleucid economic structure is entirely diachronic, and it is impossible to discern any administrative or economic patterns which can be ascribed to the early stages of organization.[19]

There is an exception to what I have been saying, the area of religion. Here little has gone unnoticed, and there even have been special studies of the religious concerns of immediate

[14]Jakob Seibert, *Das Zeitalter der Diadochen* (Erträge der Forschung 185, Darmstadt, 1983).

[15]Which appeared in three volumes (Munich) in the years 1937, 1944, 1952, 2nd edition, 1964-67.

[16]Vol. II, Nancy, 1967; 2nd edition, 1979-1982.

[17]As in V. Ehrenberg's examination of "The Hellenistic State," Part II of *The Greek State* [translation of *Der Griechische Staat*, II, *Die hellenistische Staat*, Leipzig, 1958] (London, 1960, 2nd ed. 1979).

[18]An exception is H. Seyrig's study of the commercial and economic potential of the siting of the foundations of Seleucus Nicator, "Séleucus I et la fondation de la monarchie syrienne," *Syria* 47 (1970), pp. 290-311.

[19]Heinz Kreissig, *Wirtschaft und Gesellschaft im Seleukidenreich: Die Eigentums- und die Abhängigskeitsverhälnisse* (Berlin [GDR], 1978).

successors, such as Swinnen's article of 1971 for Ptolemy,[20] or Bernd Funck's investigation of the nature and purposes of the "stadtkult" and "Staatkult" established by Seleucus I.[21] A good part of the reason for this is the interest in tracing, or arguing over, the origins of institutions better known in later times, like the worship of Sarapis or the establishment of dynastic cult. But there is also working the fact that we have some epigraphical evidence of royal activities in this area, and even more, that we learn from literary sources as divergent as Plutarch and Tacitus of specific acts in this area—Ptolemy's procurement of the statue of Sarapis from Sinope, and his construction of an appropriate temple in which to house it.[22]

The voting of royal cults by the cities and the establishment of the dynastic cults is generally seen by modern writers as political, even propagandistic in nature, although honest evaluations admit the difficulty of understanding quite how these acts achieve these goals.[23] The forms of texts honoring later kings admittedly became more formulaic than those composed earlier to honor the first rulers, and this change in style may mean that the establishments of cult were more a matter of form than genuine appreciation of royal benefit, as has been asserted. On the other hand, it may equally suggest that, as the kings became a more familiar set of figures, the great role that they played as individuals brought the cities to honor them as fixtures of the system, so to speak, rather than for specific actions. The significance of the kings to the cities may be revealed by the well-known hymn to Demetrius son of Antigonus, in which the

[20]W. Swinnen, "Sur la politique religieuse de Ptolémée 1er," *Les Syncrétismes dans les Religions Grecque et Romaine* (Colloque de Strasbourg, 9-11 June, 1971), Travaux du Centre d'Études Supérieures Spécialisé d'Histoire des Religions de Strasbourg (Paris, 1973), pp. 115-133.

[21]"Wurzeln der hellenistischen Euergetes-Religion im Reich Seleukos I," in E.C. Welskopf, ed., *Hellenische Poleis, Krise-Wandlung-Wirkung*, vol. III (Berlin, 1974), pp. 1290-1335.

[22]Tac., *Hist.* 4.83-84; Plut., *De Is. et Osir.* 28 and *Mor.* 984A.

[23]In treating this material, most writers cite Arthur Darby Nock's "SUNNAOS THEOS," *Harvard Studies in Classical Philology* 41 (1930), but, it seems to me, more in reference than in reflection, passing by Nock's profound observation (p. 61) which saw the emergence of the cults in terms of "the contemporary tendency to recognize something divine in human beings who were clearly out of the ordinary."

THE SUCCESSORS OF ALEXANDER

Athenians remark that "other gods hold themselves a great distance off, or have no ears, or do not exist or pay no attention to us, not even one, but you we see at hand, not wood, nor stone, but genuine, so we pray to you."[24] The contemporary Demochares, Athenaeus tells us, quoting the hymn, called this flattery of Demetrius, but the hymn emerged out of the treatment of the city by the king, who had just restored the democracy. The hymn does not, however, specify what benefits Demetrius had brought, but it prays that he will bring peace, and that he will overthrow the Aetolian League which not only was holding Delphi, but was plundering territories far away.

It was plausible to call Demetrius a god, and to ask that he look after the needs of the Athenians and other Greeks. It is a commonplace, again, to remark on the Greek view of the placement of humans along the continuum which stretches from the most completely divine through titans, heroes, humans of divine-human parentage, and allows for the re-location on the scale of humans whose divine nature has been discovered or revealed. People might argue about whether Alexander, or Demetrius, was in fact a god; many would at least not challenge the possibility.[25] Frank Walbank has recently emphasized the genuine quality of the veneration accorded the new kings, that it fitted into religious as well as political needs, and in a rapid survey has cited the texts which show ruler cult emerging broadly for the successors, for Ptolemy I, for Lysimachus, for Seleucus I,[26] in many cities in the Greek world. Walbank's treatment also illustrates the major shift which has taken place in our understanding of the origins of this ruler-worship, away from earlier ideas which saw it as an oriental phenomenon and now seemingly universally accepting it as fundamentally Greek in nature and basis.

---

[24]Quoted in Athenaeus, *Deipnosophistae* VI.253 d-f.

[25]Modern writers still struggle with the ancient mentality. J.R. Hamilton, for example, dealing with the call for divine honors of Alexander, in "The Origins of Ruler Cult," *Prudentia* 16 (1984), pp. 3-15), wonders whether "at this time Alexander's state of mind was abnormal." (p. 14).

[26]F.W.Walbank, "Könige als Götter: Überlegungen zum Herrscherkult von Alexander bis Augustus," *Chiron* 17 (1987), pp. 365-382.

19

THE SUCCESSORS OF ALEXANDER

The dynastic cult had some differences from this reaction to power place by place and from time to time. It was a formal structure, promoted and supported by the crown. The evidence of the deification of deceased (and then living) sovereigns first appears in Egypt as a cult of Alexander, with an eponymous priest, later expanded to include Ptolemy I and his wife, and later, successive members of the dynasty, a development shown by various priests and priestesses often named in documents as part of the dating formula. The cult was entirely Greek, having nothing to do with the long-standing Egyptian practice of accepting the king as god, although the Ptolemies responded to the Egyptian milieu by continuing earlier practice in the Egyptian temples, and even extending some of the Greek cult formulary to Egyptian practice. Although in Syria there is later evidence of the promulgation of a dynastic cult, it neither was so centralized nor so pervasive as in Egypt, perhaps because the ruler cults of the cities seemed to satisfy whatever need the dynastic cult was created to meet. In its full expression it was primarily a Ptolemaic institution, and its spread into other areas may have been due to influence or imitation of Ptolemaic practice. Its utility to the sovereign has been very difficult for moderns to understand. Bickerman has suggested that the Seleucid dynastic cult was arranged to provide an expression of religious activity for Greeks settled in new lands,[27] but in Egypt, where the dynastic cult was strongest, the crown-promoted cults of Isis and Sarapis in their Hellenized form offered an easy access to deity without the creation of another complex (and costly) priestly structure. It is very difficult to provide an explanation apart from the most modernizing and secularist conceptions of propaganda. It is not at all difficult to understand how a cult of the god Alexander might have been instituted in the first place, and it may just be the opacity of ancient religious attitudes that precludes us from understanding how that was extended to the Ptolemies as a genuine expression of religious act. If, on the other hand, dynastic cult (and ruler cult) are to be regarded as some form of propaganda, as is so often said, the universal acceptance of that thesis will wait until we have reviewed thoroughly the nature of

[27] *Institutions des Séleucides* (Paris, 1938), pp. 250-256.

THE SUCCESSORS OF ALEXANDER

propaganda in the period[28]—and seen demonstrations that some of the terms, temples, coins and cults identified as propaganda were not only launched but actually hit something. There has also been a continuing interest in defining the nature of the monarchy exercised by the successors, although with quite a difference in style between those who look at the later monarchy in terms of political theory, and those who describe it in terms of specific events and considerations which shaped it.[29] The conceptions of the monarchy exercised by the kings after Alexander depend to a significant extent on ideas about the nature of kingship of Philip II and Alexander the Great, and there is a great deal of debate over just what the nature of that monarchy was, whether the kings "represented the state," whether there was a constitutional quality to the monarchy by which the power and the options available to the king were subject to known or agreed limits,[30] whether the power of the monarchy was balanced or restricted by an "army assembly" which was formal and held sovereign power, a concept which has had great influence over the past decades,[31] whether there might have been a significant difference between most of the monarchies and that of a "national" monarchy in Macedonia itself.[32] A wholly different approach has argued that

[28]This has been an identified desideratum for fifty years, called for by W. Otto and H. Bengtson in 1938 in *Zur Geschichte des Niederganges des Ptolemäerreiches* (Abh. Bay. Akad. Wiss., Phil-.hist. Abt., Neue Folge 17).

[29]Compare, for example, Horst Braunert's "Staatstheorie und Staatsrecht im Hellenismus," *Speculum* 19 (1969), pp. 47-66, with R.M. Errington's "The Nature of the Macedonian State under the Monarchy," *Chiron* 8 (1978), pp. 77-133.

[30]This is essentially the position of N.G.L. Hammond, expressed in *A History of Macedonia* II (Oxford, 1979).

[31]The theory of Friedrich Granier, *Die makedonische Heeresversammlung*, (Munich, 1931), which argued as well that the function of the army continued into later times, a theory successfully opposed by Elias Bickerman, *Institutions des Seleucides* (Paris, 1938), pp. 8-11. Granier's thesis, although rejected by Pietro de Francesci, *Arcana Imperii* (Milan, 1948), p. 343 ff., was in the main lines accepted by Aymard and Briant (next note).

[32]This was a concept propounded to reconcile Granier's thesis with the evidence of other monarchies after Alexander, by André Aymard, *Études d'histoire ancienne* (Paris, 1967) 73-99; 100-122; 123-135;143-163; and elsewhere; followed, with a distinction between an army assembly and a people's assembly, by Pierre Briant, *Antigone le Borgne. Les débuts de sa carrière et les problèmes de l'Assemblée macédonienne* (Paris, 1973).

there is a minimum of constitutionalism in Macedonian monarchy, that this characteristic applied not only to a more or less absolute monarchy of Philip and Alexander, but pertained as well to the later monarchies as well, among which there are no essential differences of "national" or "personal" quality.[33] A recent attempt by Mooren to mediate the positions recently has returned to the view that there was a difference between the Seleucid-Ptolemaic pattern and that of other states with a Macedonian monarchy, urging that the king was not the only source of law, a view which is not exactly compromise "between the 'maximalist' and the 'minimalist' views."[34]

The tendency to treat the monarchies of Philip, Alexander, the immediate successors and then their followers as one phenomenon, albeit evolving in time, has led to attempts to reconcile items of evidence which relate in fact to quite different kings or institutions. While there has been some discussion of early views that the successors tried to find legitimization in ties with Alexander and the Argead house,[35] I do not think it has cast much light on actual conceptions of monarchy or the process of monarchic rule, beyond a general recognition that a number of the successors, notably the Seleucids and Ptolemies, emphasized the dynastic quality of the reign as the generations wore on. The treatment of these monarchies as aspects of a single institution is only partly justified by the fact that the different monarchies had some characteristics in common: the courts and court circles, initially made up of the trusted associates of the king and assembled on an ad hoc basis, but later and only in some kingdoms evincing more characteristics of bureaucracy and stability; dynastic cults and religious respect accorded to the king in most instances; conspicuous displays of wealth and patronage

---

[33]Robert Lock, "The Macedonian Army Assembly in the Time of Alexander the Great," *Classical Philology* 72 (1977), pp. 92-107, arguing that Alexander's troops exercised no constitutional authority; this line of approach takes its stand now on the discussion of R.M. Errington, note 29 above, examining all the sources in detail.

[34]Leon Mooren, "The Nature of the Hellenistic Monarchy," *Egypt and the Hellenistic World*, p. 213

[35]Most recently, and against this view, R.M. Errington, "Alexander in the Hellenistic World," *Alexandre Le Grand* (Fondation Hardt, Entretiens 22, Geneva, 1975), pp. 137-179.

in the royal centers, particularly noteworthy in Ptolemy's Alexandria; and perhaps most important of all, an attempt by the kings to accommodate themselves to prevailing ideas of kingship and to represent themselves as fulfilling expectations of both high philosophy and low followers. On the basis of the earlier concern with the theory of kingship and the existence of later tracts which are taken to trace their origins to lost works composed at the time of the successors or in the third century, scholars reconstruct an active industry composing tracts on kingship to guide or flatter the kings. Many productions of this sort there may well have been,[36] but there is, in fact, very little evidence of specific compositions or the names of putative authors working in our period.[37]

We may presume that kingship, in the period after Alexander, must have been conceived as justified in some way different from that which created Alexander king, although, no doubt, Alexander as exemplar probably controlled the conceptualizations of his successors to a considerable degree. They might be kings "like" Alexander, but they did not become kings as Alexander had, inheriting their thrones or obtaining it in some parallel to the Macedonian army practice of acknowledging an accession. In a strict sense, there had been no predecessor at all for most of them, unless Philip Arrhidaeus and Alexander IV could have been considered such in some way. Only for Ptolemy could that have really worked in a clear-cut

---

[36]There is a literary portrait of Ptolemy I claimed to have been composed in his court by Hecataeus of Abdera, its contents and its nature deduced from the contents of Book I of Diodorus. A second century text, the *Letter of "Aristeas" to Philocrates* actually survives, but its date is uncertain—it is most likely, in my view, to be toward the end of the century, and its ideas of kingship may be Jewish, to some extent, rather than based on Greek theory. Cf. D. Mendels, "'On Kingship' in the 'Temple Scroll' and the Ideological *Vorlage* of the Seven Banquets in the 'Letter of Aristeas to Philocrates'," *Aegyptus* 59 (1979), pp. 127-36.

[37] Related unattributed texts in Pack[2] do not add much: 2594, a text on kingship, could come from our period; 2597, so-called moral lessons from the careers of the Diadochi may not be a treatment of kingship; 2603, the advice to high-ranking men, the papyrus dating to III B.C., is not monarchic theory; the same applies to the similar 2591, a III text; 2573 (III) does deal with kingly virtues, but the composition may go back to the 4th century B.C., as also may the dialogue on government, 2562; a text on various political constitutions, 2570, I B.C., may not even be philosophical in nature.

manner, and then, only for the Egyptians. The successors were kings, in the first instance, because they said they were, and although they might try to behave like Alexander to show that they were kinglike, they had to function among Greeks and Macedonians in ways that would assure the recognition of their power and the acceptance of their kingly status.

Many have observed that they were not kings "of" anything,[38] and for the most part they were simply called "king." Even the notion that for Macedonia and the Antigonid monarchy there was an official royal style "king of the Macedonians" has been effectively called into question with an argument that there was, in fact "no single 'official' style,"[39] a view which, if generally accepted, will have significant implications for formalistic interpretations of the activities of the successors. I have suggested elsewhere that Alexander's kingship may be better understood in terms of the behavior of a tribal chieftain and war-leader, rather than a ruler with formal powers, more like a Viking than an administrator, and that the categories of constitutionalism, royal and subject rights and authority, really do not apply.[40] I think the evidence for this is quite good,[41] and I believe that we could understand the successors and later monarchy better if we did not try to fit our evidence into the categories we have generally used.[42]

While the generals were contending, the kings, Philip Arrhidaeus and Alexander IV, played at least a theoretical and

[38]Recently by Erich Gruen, "The Coronation of the Diadochi," *The Craft of the Ancient Historian, Essays in Honor of Chester G. Starr* (Lanham, Maryland, 1985), pp. 253-263, arguing that the meaning of "king" as taken by the diadochi was, in fact, undefined.

[39]R.M. Errington, "Macedonian 'Royal Style' and Its Historical Significance," *Journal of Hellenic Studies* 94 (1974) 37.

[40]*The American Historical Review* 93: 5 (1988) 1270-86.

[41]For example, E. Carney's "Regicide in Macedonia," *Parola del Passato* 38 (1983), pp. 260-272, also finds the Macedonian monarchy more personal than institutionalized, when she considers the examples of regicide, and finds that the attempts show personal motivations, homosexual involvements, insults and the like, rather than intentions to make political impact.

[42]The importance attributed to the army, for example, may be due to an instability in the relationship between generals and troops primarily in the first decade after Alexander's death, and it may be only the circumstances of that particular period which made it possible for the army to exercise such influence.

propaganda role, trotted out to justify actions and to summon support.[43] To the Greek cities, perhaps, the Macedonian kings were less effective as inducements or rallying points,[44] but among the Macedonians, the utility of the kings, later the lone king, as a screen for activity, may partially explain the long delay in formalizing a royal claim on the part of any of the generals. Or Alexander IV may not have been dead as early as 311 or 310, as the modern consensus has it.[45] The idea of kingship for the satraps was certainly not completely absent during the period. In Persia, in 316, Antigonus was "considered worthy of the honor of kingship by the natives as if he were the agreed lord of Asia, and he himself, sitting down with the friends made his plans about the satrapies."[46] The "royal manner" of Cassander remarked by Diodorus must also be considered, unless that, unlike the attitude of the eastern natives, is a reflection of the attitude of the historian—a possibility of significance which must be considered seriously when assessing Diodorus' evidence. Perhaps also Diodorus' writing rather than the attitude of the troops is the remark that in 312 Demetrius had a "gentleness about him fitting to a young king,"[47] but the remark that he wore royal armor and raised great expectations as a result is more significant. Indicative also that the idea was not out of people's

[43]This application of the royals began quite early, as we read in Diodorus XVIII.57 ff. of the generals calling on one another for support in aid of the kings, and Olympias herself asking for aid on her own behalf and that of the kings.

[44]Quite early, we read, for example, that in 318, after Polyperchon's failure to take Megalopolis, "most of the Greek cities, despising Polyperchon because of his worsting in the siege of Megalopolis, revolting from the kings, inclined toward Cassander." (Diod. XVIII.74.1.)

[45]Ben Zion Wacholder, "The Beginning of the Seleucid Era and the Chronology of the Diadochi," in *Nourished with Peace, Studies in Hellenistic Judaism in Memory of Samuel Sandmel* (Chico, Calif., 1984), pp. 183-211, argues on the basis of contemporary texts which accept 305/4 as the end of Alexander IV and the beginning of new regnal calculation, and claims that the Diodorus passage on which the conventional date is based has been misunderstood. Wacholder makes a good, if not ironclad case, and his work is likely to provoke a spate of discussion.

[46]Diod. XIX.48.1.

[47]Diod. XIX.81.4; and, according to Diodorus, XIX.92.5, Seleucus wrote to Ptolemy in a manner "having kingly majesty worthy of rule," a remark which may just reflect the attitude of Diodorus or his source, or may in fact be revelatory of Seleucus' behavior at the time.

minds is the oracle Seleucus received from the Branchidae, which he reported to his troops in 312 on his return to Babylonia; he claimed that the oracle had called him "King Seleucus." Later, Demetrius was addressed by the Nabataeans as "King Demetrius."[48]

Whatever the extent of the tentative explorations of the idea of kingship, it is clear that down to Triparadeisus, the armies by no means treated their generals as royal in any way, nor did the generals arrogate the notion of authority or sovereignty to themselves. Occasionally, Diodorus' favorable treatment of Ptolemy almost seems like a transposition of an Alexander-description, as he portrays Ptolemy in battle against Perdiccas in the manner we are accustomed to think of for the great conqueror,[49] and asserting, in connection with Ptolemy's honors for Alexander that "because of his grace of spirit and greatness of soul men collected from everywhere to Alexandria and eagerly furnished themselves for the campaign."[50] Nevertheless, he does not actually call him "kinglike" in these connections. It is clear that whatever ideas of kingship for the generals might have been in the air—and most in non-Greek areas—the notion of monarchy, whatever that might imply, was not yet being extended to the generals in the Hellenic sphere.

The text of Diodorus suggests that in the times that the royal titles were being assumed in 306-304, there was developing a greater aura around the leaders. It is of course in 307, on the occasion of the "liberation" of Athens and the restoration of the democracy that Antigonus and Demetrius are given their tribes, statues, crowns, altar as Saviors, and games with procession and sacrifice at Athens.[51] Rhodes, in 305, after the successful resistance of Demetrius' siege, acknowledged help by setting up statues of (now Kings) Cassander and Lysimachus,[52] and indicated the greater support of Ptolemy by enquiring of the oracle of Ammon at Siwah if they should honor him as a god.

[48]Diod. XIX.96.3.
[49]Diod. XVIII.34
[50]Diod. XVIII.28.5.
[51]Diod. XX.46.2.
[52]Diod. XX.100.2.

THE SUCCESSORS OF ALEXANDER

Upon the affirmative answer, they built the Ptolemaion.[53]

This occurred, of course, very shortly after all the leading generals began calling themselves kings. That event, which looks very large in our own account of events and strongly affects our conceptualization of the development of the monarchies, is dealt with in a surprisingly cursory manner by the sources in whom the treatment can be judged. In Diodorus, only a few lines are devoted to what we sometimes think of as a momentous event, and I may quote, to make clear just what was said:

> "And Antigonus, learning of the victory which had been achieved and quite raised up by the size of the advantage he had gained, put on a diadem and for the future used the official desigation of king, conceding also to Demetrius to obtain the same form of address and honor. But Ptolemy, in no way cast down because of his defeat, took on the diadem for himself also, and in everything he designated himself as king. And like them, the rest of the the dynasts in imitation referred to themselves as king, Seleucus, just having acquired the upper satrapies and Lysimachus and Cassander, who held the divisions which had originally been given them."[54]

The event is treated at a little more length and given a good deal more historical significance by Plutarch in his life of Demetrius.[55] The biographer tells us of the friends putting the diadem on Antigonus' head, that the new king sent one to his son with a letter addressed to "King Demetrius," that Ptolemy took the title, and so too Lysimachus and Seleucus—who had already been called such by the barbarians—while Cassander, who did not himself use the title, was accorded it in writing and speaking by others. The significance Plutarch finds in this relates to the behavior of the new kings. It was not just a style; the new monarchs were exalted by the title, and they assumed a concomitant behavior. They even treated people with more

---

[53]Diod. XX.100.3-4. Interestingly enough, Diodorus does not use the epithet "king" for Ptolemy here, although he does apply it to Lysimachus and Cassander.

[54]Diod. XX.53.2-4.

[55]Erich Gruen, note 38 above, sees the actions reported by Plutarch as a carefully staged "event."

THE SUCCESSORS OF ALEXANDER

violence. "So much strength was there in one flattering word, and it effected so much change for the world."[56] Plutarch's estimation is often our own as well, and it may be right, but the ancient treatment of events seems to suggest a more gradual development of the autocracy condemned by the philosopher-biographer of Roman times.

In some ways, I think we are still significantly affected by Plutarch's evaluation of this change in governmental style. For a long time, Plutarch's text would have been the only one commonly available to western historians, and his observations would have been effective in forming the common view of these kingships. Diodorus, who would surely not have been read much by any but specialists, would not have countered a prevailing view, and it is only the nineteenth and twentieth-century obsession with fragments and documents that can have had any significant weight against Plutarch's ideology. Plutarch's interpretation has a post-Domitianic flavor, and the evidence suggests that the new kings did not immediately launch themselves into arrogant superiority as he claimed, but that they proceeded, tentatively in some directions, to define for themselves and for their followers just what they were.

We will understand that world better if we recognize that there were a number of audiences before which the new kings had to put on their performance. There were the Macedonians and Thracians, accustomed to kingship, some with a memory of Alexander, and all, in any case, part of a tradition which expected of a man who would be king that he would demonstrate military prowess, win battles, provide loot and be generous with it, for whom kingship was perhaps hereditary to some extent, but for whom it also must be asserted and preserved with force and courage to be retained. The Greek cities had no such set of categories into which the new kings could fit themselves, and modern historians face an important issue in understanding the ideological problems which the kings presented to the cities.[57] If

[56]Plut. *Dem.* 18.2.
[57]As, for example, G.J.P. Aalders, "City State and World Power in Hellenistic Political Thought," *Actes de la VII Congrès de la fédération internationale des associations d'études classiques* I (Budapest, 1984), pp. 293-301, sees not only that the kingship needed "explanation and justification for Greek subjects" (p. 296), but that the

28

there was any royal behavior which they might use for the Greeks, it would best lie in the direction of the philosophers' kings, concepts which the leaders of the cities would recognize. So there were two images they had to present—more than two outside Greece and Macedonia, for there were the native peoples to consider. Insofar as the kings had any desire to be accepted by the natives, and it would certainly be practical to avoid native opposition, they would want to present themselves in a manner acceptable to, if not positively enticing of, a population they did not know very well, could not address in its own language or languages, and was scattered over a considerable area.

This was a very complex situation. For the new monarchs in eastern regions, the traditional native monarchies did not present much of a problem, for they could let existing institutions stand, natives follow their earlier customs, and whether the Greek-speaking monarchs or their officials understood the traditions or not, so long as the king himself was incorporated into local practice it did not matter very much what those traditions actually were. So too, traditional Macedonian attitudes required no new arrangements. As generals and satraps, the leaders had already been meeting the expectations of the troops, and as kings, they needed only to continue being as successful militarily as they could, something they would certainly want to do anyway. In the third area, touching on the concepts and expectations of the Greeks, they could apply what they knew of the ideology of monarchy which would be current in the Greek world. Their youthful training in the cultured Macedonian court would stand them in good stead here, as they presented themselves to the Greek cities as patrons of Hellenism and Greek culture. They also had Alexander's behavior as an example, in his relation to the religions of the natives and the Greeks, in the manner in which he related to Greek cities receiving cults there and representing himself as a liberator from Persian control, and they also had the pattern of his traveling circus which they might follow, to settle historians, poets, scientists and other Greek practitioners of the literary arts in their various capitals. So the successors had some examples to guide them in their

enormous difference between the nature of the king's rule and that of polis government was not very clearly perceived.

dealings with the Greek cities and the establishment of their own courts. In responding to Greek expectations of kings, the new rulers were not without resources.

If I am right that for Philip and Alexander, kingship was a kind of war-band leadership, more a pursuit of military success and booty aimed at satisfying the expectations of their followers than it was the kind of rational policy moderns have sought to discern, and this is a part of the explanations for their activities, we may be tempted to apply the same set of attitudes, at least to some extent, to the world of the successors. Is, in other words, the continual warfare as much an expression of the need of the military leaders, then kings, to demonstrate their effectiveness to the followers whom they required in order to be effective in the first place? Should we be looking for long-range policy? Is the wild adventurism of Demetrius, so self-defeating to moderns, just the extreme expression of the ambitions of a leader at the end of the fourth century? Is the nature of the settlement of Egypt by Ptolemy an exception to the rule among the successors, perhaps explicable by reference to the base on which Ptolemy found himself, rather than in the dynamics of Aegean and Mediterranean politics.? How much of military and political policy was demanded by economic considerations?

These are the kinds of broad questions which should be asked about the major events and personalities of the decades which followed immediately on Alexander's death. On another level of activity, that of life in the cities which no longer were the great influencers of history, we would like to know much more about how the city-state developed in this first period of political powerlessness. It has been conventional to pick 338 and Chaeronea as the time and place when the classical Greek city-state came to an end with Philip's victory over Thebes and Athens, but Thebans and Athenians were not quite so certain of the terminus. They certainly thought themselves free and strong enough to assert autonomy on Alexander's accession, and although the Thebans took a lesson from the conqueror, the Athenians were not ready to give up. The city state did not die with Chaeronea, nor with Alexander's dominion, nor with the establishment of the successor kingdoms. To a significant degree, what we think of as Hellenism, in its manifestations of education, creative literary, philosophical and scientific activity, continued in some of the older cities and also flourished in many of the new Hellenic foundations of the eastern Mediterranean. It is to the period of the successors that we must look to find the emergence of the common patterns of activity which marked urbanism and city-state life under the dynasts, but with some exceptions, the city as it developed in this period has not been a particular focus of interest in the most recent years.[58]

A good deal of what we know about the cities in this period comes from a wealth of inscriptional texts which emerge from the active relations between the cities and the kings or the cities with one another. Ever since these inscriptions began to be found and published, it has been clear to historians that the civic institutions of the city state continued for the most part unchanged, despite the clear evidence of royal interference with civic wishes from time to time. Most of the early texts we have come from the older cities of the Aegean. The new foundations did not have the tradition of international activity which produced much of the epigraphy of the late fourth and early third centuries, and so we do not have many inscriptions which provide insight into their workings at their inception as Greek communities. The essential Hellenism of these communities can be traced in later texts and from excavation, but we still have very large gaps in our understanding of the structure of Seleucid administration, and the manner in which the cities fitted into a bureaucracy which was quite different from the better known Ptolemaic, necessarily different, of course, for the variety of ethnic communities with which the administration had to deal and the much more difficult communications of the Seleucid realm.

If we know something about the old cities, less about the new in terms of the communal activities and their relationships with

---

[58]There have been, of course, studies of individual cities, and the four volumes edited by E.C. Welskopf, *Hellenische Poleis, Krise-Wandlung-Wirkung* (Berlin, 1974), but I am thinking primarily of synthetic works like those by Claire Préaux, "Les villes hellénistiques, principalement en Orient: leurs institutions administratives et judiciaires," in *Receuils de la société Jean Bodin* VI: *La ville 1: Institutions administratives et judiciaires* (Brussels, 1954), pp. 69-134, and "Institutions économiques et sociales des villes hellénistiques," *Recueils de la société Jean Bodin* VI: *La ville 2: Institutions économiques et sociales* (Brussels, 1955), pp. 89-135, which are now over 30 years old.

one another and to successors, we know practically nothing of the individual citizens, their activities and their movements. While the wealth of Athenian inscriptions has now made it possible for us to engage in prosopographical studies of Athenians, little has been done in this regard for texts found elsewhere. It is a commonplace to remark of the development of isopolity among Greek cities as the centuries after Alexander progress, and to assert the movement of individuals from Old Greece to the loci of activity and power in the East; there has been no significant effort to elucidate that social mobility in terms of people actually named in our texts. Admittedly, the scanty representation from the period of the successors makes that difficult for the earliest period, but later texts might permit us to see something of that period from the effects evident later. The assembly of texts which indicate the presence of foreigners in cities, as, for example, dedications at Pergamum by an Aeginetan and a Boeotian,[59] would be very useful. Tracing the movements of careerists in the service of the kings is sometimes possible, as in the case of the Timarchos son of Menedemos who in mid-second century, after serving as treasurer at Pergamum, was appointed as *neokoros* of Artemis at Sardis.[60] Funerary inscriptions also are promising indicators or resettlement.[61] In Seleucid areas in particular this close analysis would be instructive, in view of the difficulty of tracing Seleucid colonization and settlement policies and the manner in which they changed from the time of Seleucus himself down to the rulers of the mid-second century. The recognition that there was a significant movement of population, particularly in connection with the creation of armies of Macedonians, Thracians and others of Balkan origin in the East, along with the complaint that we cannot quantify this movement, suggests that we might try to squeeze more out of our epigraphical material than we have heretofore attempted. For the earliest period, and in Egypt, Bagnall has demonstrated the potential of the material, assembling the evidence which argues very persuasively that the influx of cleruchs from the Greek world

[59] *Inscr. Perg.* 48, 49.
[60] *Inscr. Sardis* 4; cf. also his dedication to Artemis, *Inscr. Sardis.* 89.
[61] See a review of the evidence for substantial percentages of gravestones of foreigners in Davies, *Cambridge Ancient History*[2] VII (1), p. 267, with citations.

into Egypt came at the very beginning of the period of Ptolemaic rule, under Ptolemy I,[62] a view that would have a significant impact on the prevailing impression that the whole period was one of migration and movement of Greeks to the east.

Quantitative studies are, of course, the vogue today. A near-century of compiling statistics from the ever-growing corpus of papyri and inscriptions has been capped by the use of the analytic capability of the computer. The availability of this tool makes it much easier for us to follow the program of the cultural materialists, attempting to build a picture of economic and social life from an aggregate of the evidence of the activities of individuals. In a period like that following Alexander, for which the documentary materials dominate in quantity over the literary, it is easy to take this approach as the path of least resistance. But in narrowing the chronological scope to the decades of the successors, we reduce the potential of the quantitative approach. As a result, evidence for the whole period, not just its first four decades of which I have been writing here is taken into the account in order to make it possible to present any kind of picture at all. And evidence from all parts of the Hellenic Mediterranean is accepted as indicators of an overall situation, this despite awareness and warnings of local differences. These local differences are, I think, much more than minor; Egypt, for all we might like to apply its wealth of papyrological evidence as paradigm, was, I think, very different from the rest of the Hellenic world, and the evidence of the distribution of immigration from different parts of the Hellenic world which can be traced there cannot be assumed to be more than local.[63] Certainly, after the successors had finished their run at administrations and the different regions of the Mediterranean had settled into the patterns first laid down, the development of each region must be traced independently of the others, and it is only after that is done that we will be in a position to rethink what we understand to be a general situation. We need, in other words, new Stracks, Bouché-Leclerqs, Bevans and Bickermans before we can hope for a new Rostovtzeff.

---

[62]R.S. Bagnall, "The Origins of Ptolemaic Cleruchs," *BASP* 21 (1984), pp. 7-20.
[63]For the distribution, see Bagnall, preceding note.

THE SUCCESSORS OF ALEXANDER

Most of all, we need to pay more attention to the successors themselves than we have done heretofore. Whether we believe they were motivated by ideas or whether we insist that their actions were determined by impersonal forces, the period of the successors is precisely that time of change in which the patterns of government, religion, social life and economic activity were established for succeeding generations. It is my own view that this period was a time of such rapid and extensive change that there were options open to leaders and individuals alike in meeting political, economic and personal problems, and that decisions taken consciously had effects at the time and for the future. Texts, therefore, are useful, I think, not only for evidence of act but of concept. A return to closer analysis of literary texts and an attempt to discern concepts behind documents may offer as much promise as quantitative analysis for the elucidation of the significant trends of the three centuries after Alexander.

III

TWO SOLITUDES

For the hundred years or so since the papyri began giving insights into the private and public lives of the Greek settlers into Egypt and the natives who thereafter had to deal with them, a fundamental topic of interest has been the relationship between the two cultures and two populations. Our understanding of those relationships has evolved with our understanding of the developments all through the Mediterranean during the three centuries after Alexander, and has gone through that same shift from conceptions of fusion to those of separateness and co-existence. At the same time, we have been particularly interested in trying to discern whether the Greek settlers exploited the native element in Egypt, or whether there was an openness and freedom available to Egyptians who wanted or had the ability to move in the Hellenic milieu. For this question, like that of fusion or separation, the wealth of documentation of public and private activity which the papyri make available for Egypt has given us the potential of answering these questions not for the intellectual class represented by literature but for more ordinary people who made up part of the population of Greek Egypt.

Ordinary people, yes, when compared to kings and politicians like Philip and Pericles, writers like Theocritus and Thucydides, but not so ordinary against the background of the illiterate masses of Egypt. It is important to recognize that almost all our evidence about the activities of Greeks and Egyptians derives from the documents of the literate business class: the genuinely literate made up no more than 20% of the population, at the most generous estimate; the propertied class which engaged in the private and official transactions recorded in our texts was probably much smaller than that. I would guess that we are looking at the society of the top 10% of the Greek-speaking population, at the most, when we treat the Greek papyrus texts, and it would be an important advance in our knowledge of Ptolemaic Egypt if we could do more than guess about the demographics of the element of the population which produced our texts. Another of Jean Bingen's perceptive and revealing discussions of the social situation has recently shown how the royal control of agriculture left an inadequate access to land, particularly wheat-producing land, to the Greek immigrants. As a result, Bingen concluded, the Greek did not become an integral part of the main economic thrust of Egypt, agriculture: "He will be a royal official, a cleruch, an agricultural entrepreneur who acts as a middleman between cleruch and peasant, a business agent who, like Zenon, is a parasite on rural society."[1] Bingen's discussion makes one of the most significant departures from earlier treatments of the evidence because its conclusions suggest that the wealth of Greek papyrus texts may be due less to great prosperity on the part of the Greeks than to their being forced into manifold commercial activities on the periphery of the main game, and it makes for a very different view of the role of the Greeks than that which has held the ground up to now.

The movement of Greeks to Egypt was a great phenomenon in the history of Hellenism. It attracted the attention of contemporary poets like Theocritus and Herondas, and it provided the opportunity for a radical transformation in the fortunes of individuals and families. It elevated, in the courts of kings and in the governments of cities throughout the east, men whose positions had earlier been either negligible or volatile in mercenary armies, and in Egypt, always a place of fascination to Greeks, it planted individuals and institutions over a vast and uncitified landscape. The Hellenic immigrants brought with them not only their military power, but also civic institutions on which they modeled even relatively small villages in remote places. That the immigrant Greeks could be described as a "privileged" class was early recognized. Not only in their assignments of billets and land in amounts which varied from vast estates held by high officials down to quite modest plots granted to ordinary soldiers who took service in Egypt, but in the whole orientation of government and culture Hellenism was dominant. The questions were not problems of identifying the tokens of Greek privilege, but rather were related to the extent to which the ruling class was accepting of Egyptians who "hellenized," and the extent to which the natives even wanted to cross over into the ruling culture. And, as was characteristic of

---

[1]"Tensions structurelles de la société ptolémaïque," *Atti del XVII congresso* III, p. 936.

TWO SOLITUDES

our analysis of so much of Ptolemaic Egypt until very recently, the evidence was read in terms of policy, as indicators of what the kings, or at least the first two Ptolemies, intended and made happen in the land which they were organizing. Rostovteff would find "nothing to show that he [Ptolemy] discriminated in principle between Macedonians, Greeks, and natives,"[2] and he saw the evolution of the relationship beween the peoples as affected by a royal policy which shifted from one of "benevolent domination" to one of "association."[3]

Royal policy, insofar as there was any, was only part of the story, and the attitudes of the Greeks outside of Alexandria who came into daily contact with the Egyptians made for a much more powerful influence on the extent to which the two cultures actually mixed. Bevan, who as one of the earlier generation saw a process of fusion at work, tried to point out how different was the situation in Egypt, where Greeks had come to stay in a land of venerable culture, from that of South Africa, where a tiny white minority imposed itself on a "primitive people," or of India, where the Europeans made up "only a transient community."[4] Bevan stressed that the Greeks, however superior they might have thought their culture, were not prone to what he called "race prejudice," and he emphasized the importance of a process of intermarriage which produced a situation in which "The distinction between the higher stratum of Greeks and lower stratum of natives did not cease, but it became more a matter of culture and tradition than of physical race."[5]

It is this relationship between Greek and Egyptian that most recent analysis has struggled with, and in social, rather than political, terms. In his recent survey of Egypt in Ptolemaic and Roman times, Alan Bowman devoted two chapters, and rather more than a third of the book, to "Poverty and Prosperity", and "Greeks and Egyptians."[6] Naphtali Lewis has devoted a special study to an analysis of families of largely immigrant or largely

---

[2]*SEHHW* I, p. 263.
[3]*SEHHW* II, pp. 706-707.
[4]Edwyn Bevan, *A History of Egypt under the Ptolemaic Dynasty* (London, 1927), p. 86.
[5]*Ibid.*, p. 87.
[6]Alan K. Bowman, *Egypt After the Pharaohs* (Berkeley, 1986), pp. 89-164.

native background to demonstrate the manner in which, with time, the native element in the population managed to assert a thrust to upward mobility.[7] And Édouard Will has called on us to recognize the colonial nature of the relationship between Greeks and natives, and has argued that modern parallels of such societies may help us to fill the gaps left by the ancient sources.[8]

The question of the mobility of the native population and the position of the immigrants to Egypt is one of great intrinsic interest to the analysis of human institutions. For the most part, our investigation of the material has proceeded in an anecdotal way through the analysis of specific incidents or cases. This method produces conclusions from which, one hopes, we may generalize. Lewis' review of the experience of several families over the whole stretch of Ptolemaic history is unusual in this regard, in that it attempts to identify trends on a larger body of evidence, but even here, the base is restricted to a small number of families. I suspect, however, that the future will bring more and more analyses in which evidence can be assessed quantitatively rather than anecdotally. This will occur because the decades since the Second World War have seen many excellent topical collections of evidence or thematic republications of texts. Lewis' analysis of the family of Dionysius, son of Kephalas, for example, was greatly facilitated by the new assembly and re-edition of all the relevant texts,[9] and his treatment of the activities of Menkhes, village scribe of Kerkeosiris in the Fayum, would hardly have been possible without the prior assembly of the evidence relating to the town and its taxes by John Shelton[10] and Dorothy Crawford.[11] Now that the demotic texts of the Zenon archive have been made available and the whole archive

[7]Naphtali Lewis, *Greeks in Egypt* (Oxford, 1986).

[8]"Pour une 'Anthropologie Coloniale' du monde hellénistique," *The Craft of the Ancient Historian, Essays in Honor of Chester G. Starr* (Lanham, Maryland, 1985), pp. 273-301.

[9]By E. Boswinkel and P.W. Pestman in *Papyrologica Lugduno-Batava* XXII (Leiden, 1982).

[10]*Tebtunis Papyri* IV, ed. J.G. Keenan and J.C. Shelton (London, 1976).

[11]D.J. Crawford, *Kerkeosiris, an Egyptian Village in the Ptolemaic Period* (Cambridge, 1971).

made accessible by a new guide,[12] that vast body of material is much more amenable to analysis as well.

Some promise is yet to be fulfilled. Although Fritz Uebel's magnificent study of the cleruchs is repeatedly consulted and cited for many purposes in studies of Ptolemaic Egypt through the reign of Ptolemy VI,[13] it has not yet been made the base of a full analysis of the activities of all these military settlers who were the foundation of the Hellenic settlement of Egypt. With all the texts relating to these individuals now collected, it would be possible to draw some conclusions about their marriage matters, their business and agricultural activities, their relative prosperity and the like, treating the whole class rather than individual members who are prominent for one or another reason. Furthermore, an extension of Uebel's work to the end of the dynasty would make possible more analysis of the land-assignments and the land-receivers as Egyptians began their movement into the ranks of army and cleruchs.

On the question of cultural influence, recent years have seen quite a significant shift of opinion away from that of earlier times. While it has always been clearly understood that in the first few generations, the settlers from Hellenic areas vigorously pursued and preserved their Greek traditions, not only in language but in other areas of culture as well, the evidence for the second and first centuries has been read to produce a story of gradual interpenetration of Greek and Egyptian ideas. Most visible to modern readers of papyri was the evidence of name change: Egyptians who took Greek names, abandoning the nomenclature of their childhood, or, alternatively, operating with dual names, the Greek name in the Greek milieu, Egyptian for the native environment. We now know, however, that the people who followed this practice were very few in number, and that the ethnic nature of a name indicated, not a predilection for cross-cultural transfer, but the ethnic milieu of the individual.[14]

---

[12]P. W. Pestman, *Greek and Demotic Texts from the Zenon Archive, Papyrologica Lugduno-Batava* XX (Leiden, 1980); *A Guide to the Zenon Archive, Papyrologica Lugduno-Batava* XXI (Leiden, 1981).

[13]F. Uebel, *Die Kleruchen Ägyptens unter den ersten sechs Ptolemäern*, Abhandlungen der Wissenschaften zu Berlin (Berlin, 1968).

[14]J. Mélèze-Modrzejewski, "Le statut des hellènes dans l'Égypte lagide: Bilan et

TWO SOLITUDES

We are also aware that there was little familiarity on the part of Greeks with Egyptian language, and we can see in our texts that it is, in general, Egyptians who knew Greek rather than bilingual Greeks who provided administrative acccess to the native population—and in any case the phenomenon of bilingualism was a limited one.[15]

While there is now a consensus which agrees that the Greeks in Egypt maintained their Hellenism in separation from a vastly more numerous native population and in the face of a visually overwhelming architectural and artistic environment, there is not much agreement about how to understand that phenomenon—or, for that matter, even on the questions to be posed in light of this new perception of the Greeks in Egypt. I have dealt with it as a matter of ideology, taking the view that the conservatism of the Greeks in Egypt was part of a fundamental Hellenic assumption that stability was preferable to change.[16] Others have tended to see the situation in political terms, regarding the cultural ambiance of Egypt as serving the needs of the sovereigns, with the Ptolemies promoting for their administrative or governmental needs the various manifestations of Hellenism—literary, civic, linguistic, artistic, scientific or religious.

Here again, it would be productive to review the evidence with very careful attention to chronology against the background of the well-known political events which affected the relations of Greeks and Egyptians with one another and with the crown— events like the enlisting of Egyptians into the forces fighting at Raphia in 217 B.C., like the recurring native revolts and re-assertion of Egyptian rulers. At the end of the third century, and more frequently in the second, Egyptians coalesced around

perspectives de recherches," *Revue des Études Grecques* 96 (1983), p. 248. For a review of the problems and issues in onomastics, see J. Bingen, "Critique et exploitation de l'onomastique: le cas de l'Égypte gréco-romaine," *Actes VII Congrès de la fédération international des associations de l'études classiques* II (Budapest, 1984), pp. 557-565, esp. 562-563.

[15]Recently observed by Willy Peremans, "Sur la bilinguisme dans l'Égypte des Lagides," *Studia Paulo Naster Oblata* II, *Orientalia Antiqua* (Leuven, 1981), pp.143-154; "Le bilinguisme dans les relations gréco-égyptiennes sous les Lagides," *Egypt and the Hellenistic World*, pp. 254-280.

[16]*From Athens to Alexandria.*

leaders of their own in a series of what have been called "native revolts," which have been interpreted as arising in significant measure from a generalized opposition to the foreign rulers. Claire Préaux argued more than 50 years ago that the domestic turmoil was due more to the exploitation of the regime as well as court politics in Alexandria and local feeling in the Thebaid, but her view has not been universally accepted, perhaps because of a reluctance to follow her in dismissing what has been seen as the most important item of evidence for native hostility. The *Oracle of the Potter*, a text appearing in papyri of the second and third centuries of our era, is often alleged to be a reflection of anti-Greek feeling by Egyptians,[17] perhaps specifically in 130 B.C., but Préaux in her most recent survey of the subject argued that it is not even sure that the text was originally written in Egyptian.[18] As Janet Johnson points out, "Egyptian texts do not contain many examples of anti-Greek feeling based on the foreignness of the Greeks."[19] Préaux suggests, stressing the economic causes of discontent, that there is a good deal of analysis yet to be made in understanding the causes of native unrest. For example, study of the role of the native priesthood shows that it was generally favorable to the Ptolemies and that Egyptian temples themselves were on occasion targets of attack. In general, Peremans has argued, tapping the prosopographical knowledge to which he himself contributed so much, friendly relations among different groups in Egypt were more the rule, and insofar as troubles arose from nationalist attitudes, these causes were secondary to resentment of the economic and social position in which the Egyptians found themselves.[20]

The attitudes of the crown and the governing Greeks are also significant. Later developments whereby native Egyptians were assigned landholdings for service in the army, albeit smaller

---

[17]Argued by Ludwig Koenen, in, *inter alia*, "Prophezeihungen des 'Topfers,'" *Zeitschrift für Papyrologie und Epigraphik* 2 (1968), pp. 178-209; "Adaptation der ägyptischen Königsideologie am Ptolemäerhof," *Egypt and the Hellenistic World*,pp.143-190.

[18]*Monde hellénistique* I, pp. 389-398, esp. 395-396,

[19]"Is the Demotic Chronicle an Anti-Greek Tract?", *Festschrift für Erich Lüddeckens zum 15 Juni 1983* (Würzburg, 1984), p. 120.

[20]W. Peremans, "Les revolutions égyptiennes sous les Lagides," *Das Ptolemäische Ägypten*, pp. 39-50.

plots for service in less-prestigious infantry units, show some tendency to trust native loyalty, at least in the instance of privileged Egyptians. But in the course of the centuries over which these developments took place, how much conscious "conciliation" can we ascribe to the crown? How much more did the Ptolemies placate the native priesthood after the troubles of the second century than they had done in the palmy days of the third? Were the political overtones of cultural policy the dominant motives for action? These questions can only be addressed by reviewing, subject by subject, reign by reign, and perhaps even place by place, the evidence for different kinds of activity. It is now possible to survey Ptolemaic temple building and repair to trace increase and contraction. We can test the extent of the incorporation of Egyptians into the hellenized elite of the civilian administration of military forces in Egypt, to see whether the "time of troubles" did in fact bring about a prominence of loyal natives which we might suppose it did. We know enough officials to determine with some safety whether Egyptians ever penetrated in any significant numbers at all into the court circle in Alexandria. And we may be able to tell from the papyri, the inscriptions and the archaeological remains whether there was any sustained royal policy of promoting Greek institutions or religious activities in the villages, towns and cities of the countryside.

There are others whose influence and activities should be evaluated in reaching an understanding of social and cultural developments in Ptolemaic Egypt, people who were neither native Egyptians nor from Greek settlements around the Mediterranean. Most numerous, and most studied, of these are the Jews, but there are others whose impact may be measurable— Syrians and perhaps even Iranians. The long interest in the Jews means that our knowledge of their place in the life of Ptolemaic Egypt is quite extensive. Investigation of the texts which relate to them has gone beyond collection to commentary and synthesis,[21] and we can see in sometimes intimate detail how "ordinary" their life was. They not only formed a near-

---

[21] *Corpus Papyrorum Judaicarum,* ed. V.A. Tcherikover and A. Fuks, 3 vols. (Cambridge, Mass., 1957, 1960, 1964); and now A. Kasher, *The Jews in Hellenistic and Roman Egypt: The Struggle for Egual Rights* (Tübingen, 1985).

autonomous community in Alexandria, but Jews lived in the countryside and Jews farmed. Allowing for the random nature of preservation, we can find Jews involved in all the activities associated with the Hellenic immigrants. Although they cannot be shown to have been in the ranks of the king's "Friends," they took part fully in the life of the countryside from the third century on. They knew and wrote in Greek, and in the contracts which emerged from their commercial activities, although they can often be identified by the appearance of particularly Jewish names, many of them carry completely Greek names and patronymics and can only be identified by the ethnic "*Ioudaios.*" As early as the last quarter of the third century Jews turn up as cleruchs, they often settled in organized communities, and some held posts in administration. In the second century, some of them came to be of much greater political importance, as Jewish military officers served Ptolemy VI and his queen, Cleopatra II. An immigrant, Onias, commanded a military detachment, obtained land upriver on which he could settle his troops, and built a temple there. The generals Dositheos and Onias were the highest commanders for Cleopatra II during some of her conflicts with her brother, Ptolemy VIII, Euergetes II, and came to her rescue militarily on one occasion, while the sons of Onias later served Cleopatra III. It is the "pro-Philometor" policy of the Jews (and the "philo-Jewish" policy of Ptolemy VI) that is seen to have generated a brief flash of official anti-Semitism and a short and unsuccessful pogrom on the part of Euergetes II.

All this has been given a great deal of attention, particularly in light of the "Letter of Aristeas to Philocrates," which is now dated to the later second century B.C., when the Jewish optimism about assimilation could look back on the importance of Jews to Ptolemy VI, and even the recently-hostile Euergetes II was friendly enough to be receiving dedications on synagogues. We are, however, less informed about the critical period from the end of the second century B.C. to the time of Philo, when members of the Jewish community extended their Hellenism and its attempts to involve themselves in the life of the Greeks in the gymnasium and even in politics. The events of the riots in Alexandria in 38 A.D treated three years later in the letter of Claudius to the Alexandrians capped the development of the relationship between the Greek and Jewish Alexandrians from the third century B.C. on, and we need evidence about the last century of that development in order to comprehend the events which Philo and Josephus chronicle so vividly.

It would also cast light on the maintenance of distinctions between Greeks and Egyptians if we knew better how Syrians and Iranians fitted into the social matrix of Egypt. For the problems involved, the ethnic *"Perses"* or *"Perses tes epigones,"* is a case in point. Can anything Iranian be made of that? There is no doubt that at the end of its evolution, the term *"Perses tes epigones"* was a legal fiction assumed by a debtor because it allowed his creditor faster legal process. Scholars argue vigorously, however, over the meaning of the term in early Ptolemaic Egypt, and some believe it was assumed to indicate descent in the military class,[22] while other take it as a fictional ethnic assumed by Hellenizing Egyptians.[23] As to its origin, did I guess rightly when I speculated that the ethnic may have been used by genuine Greeks whose families had been in Egypt in Persian times and who thus had no claim to a "genuine" Greek ethnic?[24] Determination of the meaning of the term must certainly have some effect on our understanding of the simple *"Perses,"* of whom there are many attestations—with Greek names—as soldiers and cleruchs. In general, papyrologists have no expectations that these "Persians" or "Persians of the descent" have anything at all to do with genuine derivation from the Iranian area, but the use of the term may have something to do with attitudes towards the earlier Persian overlords, and any who might have remained in Egypt. At any rate, the problem remains unsolved.

Non-Jewish Semites were also known in Egypt. At the time of Ptolemy I, Philocles, the Sidonian king, held very high rank during the period's military and political manoeuvering. Doubtless, he was completely hellenized, but he was a Sidonian, nevertheless. There are also the group of Idumaeans attested at Memphis at the end of the second century.[25] Then there are

---

[22]P.W. Pestman, *Aegyptus* 23 (1963), pp. 15-53.

[23]J.F. Oates, *Yale Classical Studies* 18 (1963), pp. 5-129.

[24]A.E. Samuel, *Proceedings of the Twelfth International Congress of Papyrology* (Toronto, 1970), p. 448, n. 12.

[25]Dorothy J. Thompson Crawford, "The Idumaeans of Memphis and the

dubious characters like the Syrian lady Elaphion, who was carrying on some kind of activity in the garrison town of Elephantine in the third century, and Syrians like the slaves which Zenon papyri tell us were imported to Egypt. Some Semitic-named people found their way into positions of at least minor importance. Such was the Bithelminis of *P.Yale* 33 = *P.Hib.* 44 who held the rank of hegemon of *machimoi*—native soldiers. There is some difficulty in distinguishing between Jews and non-Jews with Levantine names, and the references to the Syrian villages in our papyri may not be discriminating between Jews and non-Jews. All in all, our knowledge of these immigrants from the Levant, and any others from points east is rudimentary, and we have very little idea of the extent of such a migration, and whether the immigrants had any impact on the social or status situation of Egypt. Nevertheless, the Levantines, and particularly the Jews, are especially interesting, for they provide a rare example of the impact of Hellenism on non-Greeks. As they turn up in our papyri, either cleruchs or civilians who joined the migration to Ptolemy's Egypt in search of fortune, they are well Hellenized. As early as the third century, most of them use Greek names, even if they preserve a parent's Semitic nomenclature, and the third-century Septuagint translation of the Hebrew scriptures was clearly made for the needs of Jews who retained their religion but had lost their language in favor of Greek. Some Jews who thought about this assimiliation were optimistic about it, for the thrust of the second-century "Letter of Aristeas" is clearly an endorsement of Jews fitting into Ptolemaic society. As I noted above, we lose track of this group until we meet Philo a century later, but it clearly remained vigorous, an example of a group which retained the essence of its beliefs while adopting cultural Hellenism extensively.

This phenomenon seems not to have been the Egyptian experience, nor did the Greeks in Egypt take much from their cultural environment. As I emphasized a few years ago, the Greeks maintained their culture in Egypt in almost complete separation from the surrounding milieu, preferring even Greek

Ptolemaic *Politeumata," Atti del XVII congresso* III, pp. 1069-1075.

literature of pre-Alexandrian time to the local and contemporary productions of Alexandria.[26] Much the same was true for religion. While the notion of "syncretism" of Greek and Oriental themes in religion is hard a-dying, the evidence goes very much against it, at least in any significant sense. While Greeks accepted the divinities they encountered in the East (as they had always been willing to worship newly found deities), their conceptualization and cult practices remained entirely Hellenic.[27] This conservative quality of Hellenism is now more and more being recognized, and the changing perspective of the impulses which drove Greek culture in Egypt in the three centuries of Ptolemaic rule call for reassessments of many aspects of that culture. Egypt was the springboard for many features of Hellenism in late Ptolemaic and Roman times; Greek culture there did not remain static, even if it took its impulses from change out of its own tradition rather than for the "oriental" environment. Thus we need to trace, in terms of Hellenism and not imagined "eastern" influences, the development of Greek literature, religions, science, and philosophy, so that we understand what sort of Hellenism was so influential in the critical centuries which saw the rise (and Hellenization) of Christianity. It is time, for example, that we understand how so important a tradition as Stoicism arose from Greek ground, and stop trying to graft it onto eastern roots with an insistence on seeing a Semitic background for Zeno of Citium.[28]

The same fidelity to its traditions shows on the Egyptian side. As the art and architecture of Egyptian temples remained almost untouched by Hellenic influences, so the Egyptians kept cult and religious practice insulated from Greek. It is well known that priestly service is almost complete separated on ethnic lines, Greeks serving as priests in Greek cult but almost never in Egyptian, Egyptians in turn rarely crossing out of their

[26]*From Athens to Alexandria*, pp. 67-74.
[27]*Ibid.*, 75-101.
[28]As we still find in Giovanni Reale, *Storia della filosofia antica* III, I sistemi dell' età ellenistica (Milan, 1976), p. 305, calling Zeno "un giovane di razza semitica," and which John R. Catan renders as "Jewish origin" (!) in the 1985 translation of Reale's work, *A History of Ancient Philosophy* III, *The Systems of The Hellenistic Age*, p. 209. I owe this reference to Joseph Bryant.

tradition into Greek. As more demotic texts become available, we can see a little more of the activities of the Egyptians in their own environment, and although there are some instances of cross cultural activity, is seems very sparse on the basis of the texts available so far,[29] and unless the currently available Egyptian material is very unrepresentative of the texts not yet published, the separation in religious areas is likely to be confirmed when we have more evidence. In general, the extensive literature in demotic which persists and grows during Ptolemaic times shows the vigor of the native tradition, and its literary activity was not in the least impeded and, so far as we can see, little affected by the presence of Hellenism. That some Egyptians rose high in the bureaucracy is also attested, and the demotic documents show both prosperity and land-ownership on the part of some Egyptian families.[30] Others are found as early as the third century operating in Greek, entrepreneurs at some level like the Greeks themselves.[31] It is also clear that these wealthier Egyptians often chose to maintain their business activities in accordance with Egyptian legal practice, a separation made possible by the Ptolemies providing for the co-existence of the two systems of law. The intensive work on demotic documents has been one of the most important developments of recent years. Not only have major archives now been published,[32] but the assembly and integration of demotic materials with Greek, as in the cases of the Zenon Archive and lists of eponymous priests, have helped bridge the gulf between Greek and Egyptian evidence, although, as Willy Clarysse has recently pointed out, there are still many

---

[29]The problems of the Demotic material and citations of some of the texts revealing the activities of the Egyptians can be found in J. Quaegebeur, "Cultes Égyptiens et Grecs en Égypte," *Egypt and the Hellenistic World*, pp. 301-324, and "Documents égyptiens et rôle économique du clergé en Égypte hellénistique," *State and Temple Economy in the Ancient Near East* II, pp. 708-729, and discussions cited by Quaegebeur.

[30]As demonstrated by W. Clarysse, "Egyptian Estate Holders in the Ptolemaic Period," *State and Temple Economy in the Ancient Near East* II, pp. 731-743.

[31]T. Reekmans, "Archives de Zénon: Situation et comportement des entrepreneurs indigènes," *Egypt and the Hellenistic World*, pp. 323-390.

[32]For instance, the texts discussed by P.W. Pestman, "L'Ambiente indigeno dell' età tolemaica," *Egitto e Società Antica*, pp. 147-161.

slips generated by the fact that parallel Greek and demotic texts are often edited at different times by different people.[33] The appearance of legal material has given us a better understanding of Egyptian law and its maintenance in Ptolemaic Egypt, and the texts have made it possible for us to develop some detailed knowledge of specific families whose vigor and prosperity would have been undetectable in the Greek papyri.

The demotic documents and Egyptian society lie before us almost as a new land for discovery. Comparisons between concepts in demotic literature of the Ptolemaic period with those of the Egyptian milieu of the Nag Hammadi Coptic texts suggest that such a fundamental change in the understanding of the nature of man as the shift from characteristic Near Eastern monism to a Hellenic dualism took place after the end of the Ptolemaic dynasty.[34] With many more documents available from recent excavations, and a large number of literary texts still to be published, there is every reason to expect to learn much more than we now know about the life of the upper class Egyptians in Ptolemaic Egypt. We will be able to support with conviction or to refute what appears to be true from the evidence currently available, that the Egyptians—even upper class Egyptians—were not much touched by Greek culture, even though in a general way, some writers in Egyptian were aware of themes in other literatures of the Near East. We will be able much better to see whether indeed the two dominant peoples of Egypt, the Greeks and the natives, remained in their two solitudes for the long period of Ptolemaic rule, and we may be able better to understand just how Egyptian culture evolved so that it could take on Christianity as the Greek texts which created Christianity for the rest of the world were translated into Coptic. More study of demotic literature should increase our understanding of the extent and the process by which Egyptian Christianity became characteristically Greek rather than Egyptian.

What we will not have from new texts, however, is insight into the situation of the masses of Egyptians who remained as

[33]"Bilingual Texts and Collaboration Between Demoticists and Papyrologists," *Atti del XVII congresso* III, pp. 1345-1353.

[34]M. Lichtheim, *Late Egyptian Wisdom Literature in the International Context: A Study of Demotic Instructions*, (Orbis Biblicus et Orientalis 52, Göttingen, 1983), pp.184-195.

TWO SOLITUDES

they always had been, poor, peasants, illiterate. For these
millions, as for an unknown number of Greeks whose families
did not succeed in Egypt, only the tax receipts and the fabled
wealth of Ptolemy attest their presence. To understand the bottom
70 or 80 percent of the population we must develop some creative
means of using our evidence to learn something about them.[35]
We would like to know how much upward mobility existed, in
fact, for people born into the peasant life. And we would like to
know if, at this level, at least, the Greeks in Egypt merged with
the vast mass of Egyptians, to bridge, at least at that level, the two
solitudes in which the cultured carried on their separate lives.

[35]The way is pointed by a study like that of Sergio Daris, "I Villaggi dell'Egitto
nei papiri greci," in *Egitto e società antica.*

IV

THE MACEDONIAN ADMINISTRATION
OF EGYPT

When Ptolemy Soter, the first of the dynasty, died in 283, he left as heir his son Ptolemy, later to be known as Philadelphus. Ptolemy II had been associated on the throne with his father two years before the old general died, and there was no difficulty in the transfer of power. It is to Philadelphus' reign, from 285 to 246, that we look for the major activities of organizing and structuring the Greek administration of Egypt, and it is Philadelphus who has received either credit for progressive government or blame for draining the resources of the country. For the most part, the second Ptolemy has held the repute which Rostovtzeff's authority provided for him, and specialists and general historian alike repeat the words or ideas of the master:

> We see the new organization partly at work, partly in the making, in the hands of Ptolemy Philadelphus. . . . In it two systems were to be blended, so as to form one well-balanced and smoothly working whole: the immemorial practice of Egypt and the methods of the Greek state and the Greek private household. . . . On the one hand it endeavored through a stricter and more thorough organization to concentrate the efforts of the people on an increase of production. On the other, it sought to develop the resources of the country by the adoption of the technical improvements that had come into use in other parts of the civilized world. . . .[1] The economic reforms and other measures of the first Ptolemies produced wonderful results.[2]

Rostovtzeff's assessment of the economy and society of Egypt has stood for the nearly fifty years since it appeared because it rested on an assembly and control of the evidence in scope and depth which had never been reached before him and has not been approached since. But now, in the last quarter of the century, aspects of this appraisal are coming into question by those familiar with the sources, the material known to Rostovtzeff

[1]*SEHHW* I, p. 272.
[2]*SEHHW* I, p. 407.

and newer texts and archaeological finds which have come to light since 1940. Claire Prèaux demonstrated in articles[3] and in her *Monde Hellénistique* of 1978 that the idea of technical improvement must be abandoned. I argued in 1983 that a genuine increase in production was not even conceived;[4] then in 1984 Eric Turner denied that Philadelphus' reform "produced wonderful results."[5] All that is left unchallenged about Philadelphus' reform is the idea that it emerged, however piecemeal, out of the program of the king and his associates in Alexandria and that it was centrally controlled. That concept may also need some modification.

The thirty-five years during which Philadelphus ruled Egypt marked a transition for Greek settlement in Egypt. While he continued as long as he could his father's policy of intervention in the Aegean area, two significant defeats of his fleet and a changed political situation abroad brought a different relationship between sovereign and subjects than that which had obtained during Alexander's reign and that of Ptolemy I. That different relationship developed concurrently with the establishment of a wide-ranging Greek-speaking bureaucracy in Egypt, an extensive series of regulations for affecting the economic life of the country, and an accommodation of Egyptian religious and legal practice which allowed the natives to carry on their lives for the most part in the manner to which they were accustomed, while at the same time the Macedonians and Greeks in Egypt related themselves intimately in many ways to the land and its gods.

While some of the structures of Ptolemaic Egypt may have owed their inception to the first Ptolemy, it is the second who was responsible for the issuance of a large number of texts dealing with economic and administrative activity in Egypt, and it is in the reign of Philadelphus that we can see the way in which Egypt was so exceptional in the Mediterranean world

---

[3]Claire Préaux, "Époque Hellénistique," *Third International Conference of Economic History* 1965 (The Hague, 1970), pp.41-74; "Sur la stagnation de la pensée scientifique à l'époque hellénistique," *Essays in Honor of C. Bradford Welles* (New Haven, American Stdies in Papyrology I, 1971), pp. 235-250.

[4]*From Athens to Alexandria.*

[5]*CAH*[2] VII,1, pp. 118-159.

after Alexander. Royal monopolies in essential materials like salt and oil, the activity of Greeks, Macedonians and others from the Aegean throughout the countryside and in complete divorce from the usual Hellenic city-state structures, the exploitation of royal lands and the rents and taxes which they produced, and the very complex bureaucracy which dealt with many aspects of the land and produce and the regulations issued by the crown created a pattern of life which for Hellenes in Egypt was very different from that experienced by those in other parts of the Mediterranean and Near East.

Ever since the publication of *Papyrus Revenue Laws* at the end of the last century, scholars have used that and texts found subsequently to explicate a conception of the economy of Ptolemaic Egypt as centrally controlled. However modern scholars interpret the effects of the organizing activity of the first half of the third century, almost all agree that Philadelphus (and his father before him) took over as much as they could of pre-existing administrative structures, and made changes only when this was essential to permit their own control of the society and economy.[6] This is a critical point, and a demonstration of the extent of any relationship between early Ptolemaic and Persian administration would help a great deal in understanding just what it was that the first two Ptolemies did do in organizing their new territory. Unfortunately, most classicists do not control the Egyptian or Persian material which relates to this question, and for the most part we depend upon the results of Egyptologists and orientalists, a problem of scholarship which has often been noted but little done for its solution. In any case, and even worse, the evidence for the Persian administration of Egypt seems to be particularly exiguous, and for the most part, Ptolemaic dependence on earlier Egyptian patterns must be deduced from Saite and earlier material. As a result, the near-unanimous assessment of "continuance where possible" remains for the most part a hypothesis, although one so reasonable in the circumstances that it will doubtless continue unless it is challenged by detailed new information.

[6]This is, in essence, Rostovtzeff's dictum, *SEHHW* I, pp. 263, 272-3, and elsewhere, and, although there is no evidence to confirm (or refute) it, it is the accepted view.

THE MACEDONIAN ADMINISTRATION OF EGYPT

For a long time the extensive documentation for third-century Egypt led to conceptions of comprehensiveness and foresight in the creation of a centrally controlled economy. Ideas of "planned economy," "monopolies," and "economic rationalism" dominated modern accounts. I have no doubt that there was some planning, some central direction and even some rationalism in the devising of administrative structures in the third century, and that Philadelphus and his staff made a considerable effort to ensure the flow of agricultural products and coin revenues to Alexandria. However, the most recent studies reflect an approach to the evidence for this activity which sees it much more in terms of ad hoc arrangements. Even the most detailed sets of regulations are now thought to have been informal in their nature,[7] in that they responded to individuals anxious to know the rules rather than to the desire of the administration to set them out. Certainly, in terms of our own knowledge of the administration created in the course of the reign of Ptolemy II, most of what we know and write about procedure and rules emerges from information conveyed in an informal way, from letters, complaints, petitions, agreements and the like, in which individuals related to one another and to officials. Certainly my own recent consideration of the material has led me to change my earlier view, in that I see the bureaucracy as more-or-less out of control and self-moving even as early as Philadelphus' reign.[8]

That the bureaucracy was elaborate, that there were separations according to the nature of the duties involved, with financial, scribal and supervision of actual agricultural activities assigned to different divisions, is obvious from our texts. The papyri of Zenon, estate-manager for Apollonius, the Alexandrian finance official who held a 10,000 aroura *dorea* in the Fayum, contains a vast amount of detail on everyday agricultural and

---

[7]The *Revenue Laws Papyrus*, for example, by Jean Bingen, *Le papyrus Revenue Laws - Tradition grecque et adaptation hellénistique* (Rhenisch-Westfälisch Akademie der Wissenschaften, Vorträge G 231, 1978).

[8]I deal with this more extensively in my paper, "The Ptolemies and the Ideology of Kingship," delivered at the Symposium on Hellenistic History and Culture, at the University of Texas at Austin, in October, 1988, and planned for publication.

financial operations in the chora in the mid third century B.C. Because there are texts which show Zenon's principal, Apollonius, in touch with the king,[9] and on occasion relaying royal ideas or instructions,[10] the correspondence as a whole has led to the assumption that Apollonius, as *dioiketes*, was "the manager in the name of the king of the economic life of Egypt,"[11] and that the activity the Zenon correspondence reflects is indicative of the king's objectives. Citing evidence that there may have been a plurality of officials with this title later in the third century and that later a *dioiketes* had a relatively low honorary rank, Turner has argued that Apollonius ranked no better than sixth at court, and perhaps as low as tenth.[12] We must, therefore, no longer assume that the activity of Zenon and Apollonius in the Fayum is representative of Egypt as a whole, or that it represents central royal direction.

In reality, the texts which relate to the king would seem to argue against coherent royal organization. We have a large number of texts which record orders, *prostagmata* as the Greek puts it, of the kings, from Philadelphus on. Although the majority of these are mined from documents which are collections of regulations or procedures, there is not a single royal order which is itself a comprehensive regulation,[13] or which even refers to such a thing. Indeed, for the most part, the royal orders would not even have been preserved, had they not been repeated, reported or recopied for private or individual purposes. It is not uncommon to find attached to an order the name or names of minor personnages who pass it on, and in one case, to Zenon

---

[9]As in *P.Cairo Zen.* 59541, attending the king's birthday celebration, *P.Cairo Zen.* 59075 and 59076, relaying gifts from a sheikh in the Ammonitis, Palestine, *P.Cairo Zen.* 59241, showing Apollonius present as escort of Ptolemy's daughter Berenice to Syria for her marriage to Antiochus, and other texts.

[10]In fact, in substantive agricultural matters, royal direction is rare, as in *P.Cairo Zen.* 59155, which states that the king had asked Apollonius to have the land sown twice in a growing season.

[11]M.I. Rostovtzeff, *A Large Estate in Egypt in the Third Century B.C.* (Madison, 1922), p. 16.

[12]*CAH*² VII,1, p. 143.

[13]The idea of the comprehensive regulation may be valid for the legal system, if there was a single, unified "diagramma judiciaire," as argued by J. Mélèze-Modrzejewski, "Le Document grec dans l'Égypte ptolémaïque," *Atti del XVII congresso* III, p.1178.

who has by the time of the text become a completely private person.[14] That we have a *Corpus des ordonnances des Ptolémées* compiled by a modern scholar out of very disparate kinds of texts should not mislead us into thinking that the Greeks in Egypt ever had such a thing. Everything, in fact, suggests the opposite: the often unofficial and even random copying of the orders; the fact that they deal in general with quite specific and individual matters; that they emerge often in response to petitions from below rather than out of "legislative" planning. Insofar as the king directed the bureaucracy, he did so by responding ad hoc to events, rather than by comprehensive planning and regulation.

Finally, we have one specific and certain instance in which a new text overturns an aspect of the earlier belief in a centrally directed agricultural economy. For a long time it was thought that the term *diagraphe tou sporou* or "regulation in regard to sowing" referred to a procedure in which the crown "regulated the cultivation according to the planned economy of the State."[15] Only in the last three decades have texts emerged that demonstrate the reverse:[16] at the local level, the schedule of intended sowing was compiled on the basis of the year's inundation by the Nile, and that document, which reflected expectations from below rather than orders from above, was submitted to the higher bureaucracy, presumably for use in regard to subsequent tax collection.

All this required a complex bureaucracy and needed some kind of supervision, and our texts show many ways in which supervision was maintained or attempted. There are requirements that officials from distinct branches be present when their concerns were affected by specific activities, as in regulations which deal with tax-farming; the records of sowing and yield are to be broadly known so that the chance of cheating is reduced. There are provisions for complex accounting

[14]*C.Ord. Ptol.* 27; see also 5 and 6 in Marie-Therèse Lenger, *Corpus des ordonnances des Ptolémées* (Brussels, 1964).

[15]Rostovtzeff, *SEHHW* I, p. 279.

[16]*P. Yale* 36, confirmed, in my view, by the so-called "Karnak Ostrakon," discovered in 1969/70 and published in translation in 1978 (E. Bresciani, "La Spedizione di Tolemeo II in Siria in un Ostrakon Inedito da Karnak," *Das Ptolemäische Ägypten*, pp. 31-37), which calls for a survey of the state of the agricultural situation.

procedures and balancing of accounts, for registrations of land and for control of implements to avoid illegal manufactures. We have a document later in the third century which we believe to have emanated from high authority setting forth advice to an important official in the countryside including specific directions for inspections and supervision.[17] But none of these assert that they are in themselves comprehensive law, although some include royal orders for information. They are, in fact, documents drawn up by the bureaucracy for the use of the bureaucracy, and they may serve private needs as much as public or official purposes.

These terms, "private, public, official," may not, however, be appropriate to the situations which we describe by them. The issue of the extent of the "private" or "state" quality of the Ptolemaic economy has been important in conceptualizing the Ptolemaic monarchy, and it has been equally significant in evaluating how individuals functioned in an environment which has been thought to presuppose the ownership of all land by the king as his "private" property. That we conceive of the Egyptian situation in terms of modern distinctions is at least partly due to an inevitable mental act of converting Greek terms to supposed equivalents in modern languages. Terminology for land-holding illustrates the point. While in his discussion of the organization of Egypt under Ptolemy II, setting out the divisions of land into *gé basiliké, gé en aphesei, gé hiera, gé en suntaxei, gé klerouchiké, gé en dorea, ktémata* and *gé idioktétos*[18] ("royal land, released land, temple land, land in assignment, cleruchic land, gift land, estates and private land," to give the usual translations). Rostovtzeff begins his survey with an acknowledgement that the terminology was not precise, the whole conceptualization of land assignments and the evolution of the Ptolemaic land-tenure system is predicated on a distinction between "private" land, as *gé idioktétos* is translated, with the houses, vineyards and gardens called *ktémata* also conceived as private, and the other classes of land which Rostovtzeff (like others) explains by reference to the terminology.

---

[17]*P. Tebt.* 703.
[18]*SEHHW* I, pp. 276-291.

THE MACEDONIAN ADMINISTRATION OF EGYPT

The issue is important, expressed in these terms, since some of the categories of land were provided to Greeks, Macedonians and other immigrants to Egypt, in order to furnish them with resources. The *doreai*, or "gift estates," were grants of extensive tracts of land to senior officials in the government, and lesser officials also received smaller grants, which fell into the category of "released land." In the same category was the "cleruchic land," set tracts which were assigned to military settlers which provided the major portion of income to the soldiers in the Ptolemaic army. These grants made it possible to support the army without great outlays in cash. These land grants were scattered about the countryside, and the effect of this system of assignment of land meant that the soldiers too were scattered onto the land, in and near the small villages and towns characteristic of the countryside of Egypt. The cleruchs who obtained these allotments paid taxes on the land, and, so far as we can see, were not considered "owners" of the land, in that the cleruchies were neither alienable nor inheritable. Such, at least, we believe to have been the concept of these grants, and of the *doreai* and other grants to civil administrators as well.

There is evidence, however, of sons carrying on the cleruchies of their fathers, and modern comments on the evolution of the land-holding system usually observe that with time, the cleruchic grants tended to be treated as "private" property which could be passed on in inheritance.[19] The issue of the manner in which "private" property existed and increased in the Ptolemaic system arises, I think, more from our notion of meaning of the terms. *Gé idioktétos* is better translated "land held personally," rather than as "private" or "privately held land," and with the change in translation, many modern conceptions about the nature of such land evaporate. The various categories of land do not classify the various land-holdings on two sides of a great divide which separates "private" from "public," or "state," but are rather meant to designate responsibility for working the land and paying taxes according to various regulations. Royal land had no direct intermediaries between officials and the farmer; temple land, *doreai* and the like presented some

---

[19]Quite early, as in *P.Lond.Zen.* 2016 (241 B.C.), we see cleruchic land formally bequeathed.

58

intermediaries, while cleruchic land invested a personal holder not only with privileges and profit but responsibilities.

The elimination of the great conceptual divide between "public" and "private" in the classification of land would go far, I think, toward reorienting our thinking about the Ptolemaic economy and the reaction of the population to it. Issues like the extent to which Greeks might have been troubled by the kings taking the territory of Egypt as their "private property" disappear, and the tendency for individual plots of land to fall into the alienable control of individuals easy to understand. Beyond this abstract change in our thinking about Ptolemaic Egypt, there are areas of a more practical nature which, if recent arguments are accepted, will significantly modify our ideas about that society. Whatever terminology may be, Bingen's observations about the limited availability of land to the Greeks shows how his "tensions structurelles" pushed the Greeks to all kinds of activities which were contrary to the interests of the crown.[20] I have argued elsewhere that the money economy in Egypt was a much smaller part of the life of the working peasantry than has hitherto been assumed,[21] and that overall, the idea that there was a "progressive" application of new technology aimed at expanding production runs counter to the evidence.[22] If we push our reevaluation of third-century B.C. Egypt even further along the road on which are already moving, and add to these considerations the idea that Greeks in Egypt of that period lacked a clear idea of "state" versus "private" interest, we will eventually develop quite a different picture of Ptolemaic Egypt from the conventional portrait of a planned society using large numbers of immigrant Greeks for the administration of a new kind of national state.

We should pursue the developing idea that administration under Philadelphus was not the rationally planned structure into which we have been trying to fit what are in reality unfittable and disparate pieces of an arrangement put together largely ad hoc, created not just by the central authority but also developed on

---

[20] "Tensions structurelles de la société ptolémaïque," *Atti del XVII congresso* III.
[21] "The Money Economy and the Ptolemaic Peasantry," *BASP* 21 (1984), pp. 187-206. See also the remarks of É. Will (note 8, Chapter III above), pp. 291-292.
[22] *From Athens to Alexandria,* pp. 45-61.

the land by officials who were pursuing their own interests at the same time as they worked to meet the crown's demand for revenue. If a strain was imposed on the population by this structure, I suggest that it might have been created by the nature of the burgeoning bureaucracy itself, rather than primarily because of the needs of the king himself. Thus, the political problems which became apparent within Egypt after the first successful campaigns of Euergetes upon his accession in 246 were, in essence, insoluble, because they were structural.

The general satisfaction all round evinced by the Canopus Decree, congratulating the king on his victory, expressing thanks for his benefactions like recapturing the statues of the Egyptian gods, and establishing a series of cult provisions to honor the royal family shows no awareness of troubles in the realm which were to become noticeable in the next reign. Whether or not Philopator's use of Egyptian forces to achieve his victory over Seleucid troops at Raphia in 217 was a direct contributor to self-confidence on the part of the native Egyptians, as has often been said, there is no doubt that at the end of his reign and then on into that of the next king, Ptolemy V, Epiphanes, native revolts were serious threats. First a native ruler, Hurgonaphor, was recognized in Thebes from 206 B.C. on, and then his successor, Chaonnophris, ruled in Thebes until 186 B.C.[23] In the same period, government in Alexandria was largely in the hands of court officials, like the Sosibius who was largely responsible for the assembly of the forces which were successful at Raphia. For much of the latter part of the reign of Ptolemy IV, and for the early part of the reign of the minor, Ptolemy V, the court circle at Alexandria was the effective government there.

For over sixty years, after the death of Ptolemy V in 180, Egypt was torn by strife. There were regencies like that for the child who succeeded as Ptolemy V, there was invasion from Syria by Antiochus IV in the years 170 to 168, there were internal dynastic quarrels, expulsions and returns of rulers, as well as occasional coalitions among members of the royal house, and

[23]For the dates, names and bibliography on this revolt, see K. Vandorpe, "The Chronology of the Reigns of Hurgonaphor and Chaonnophris," *Chronique d'Égypte* 71 (1986), pp. 204-302.

there was even a full-scale and sustained revolt in 131-130, in which Cleopatra II, the sister-wife of the reigning Ptolemy VIII set herself up in Thebes, where the documents indicate that she was recognized as ruler. Euergetes himself was briefly expelled from Alexandria during the period, and the ferocity of the conflict—or his personality—is exemplified by the kind of outrageous conduct which ancient sources like to report: the killing and dismemberment of the son he had had by Cleopatra II, and the despatch to her of the pieces of the boy's body in a box as a birthday present. The reign of Ptolemy VIII ended in 116 with Euergetes' death in June; Cleopatra II died a few months later, and a new reign, with its own personal and dynastic quarrels, began as Cleopatra III, Euergetes' second wife, ruled jointly with her son by Euergetes, known as Soter II, Ptolemy IX.

It is to this long period of dynastic conflict and supposed disruption in administration that we credit an attempt at reorganization which reaches its fullest expression in the noted amnesty of 118 B.C., the royal decree known as *P. Tebtunis 5.* By the time this forgiveness of misdeeds, remissions of debts to the crown, declaration of benefits and grants appeared, the pattern of royal *philanthropa* had become established; the joint declaration of 118 B.C. by Euergetes II, Cleopatra II and Cleopatra III is taken as a vigorous attempt to reestablish order and revivify the economic and administrative life of the countryside after so long a period of strife amongst the rulers. We depend to a significant extent on *P. Tebt.* 5 for evidence of administrative developments during this long period. There is certainly nothing like the quantity of texts of the third century on which to base our knowledge of the period, although some conclusions can be drawn from the texts of the Serapeum recluses published by Wilcken,[24] and a recent collection of administrative texts suggests that the bureaucracy functioned comfortably through some of the most difficult periods of the first half of the second century.[25] The relative scarcity of administrative texts from that period may be no more than an accident of discovery or preservation. There is certainly indication in the Tebtunis text, however, of a period of conflict and of damage done to buildings and land, and the provisions of

[24]As the collection known as *Urkunden der Ptolemäerzeit.*
[25]*Papyri Helsingienses* I, ed. J. Frösen *et al* (Helsinki, 1986).

the decree also deal with official misbehavior, prohibiting, for example, *strategoi* and others from forcing the peasants to work for their private benefit or to provide or feed livestock for their own gain or for sacrifice. There are provisions for the co-existence of Egyptian and Greek legal procedure which are taken as a conciliation of native Egyptian sentiments, and prohibitions against arrest or personal control for private debt. Administrative provisions like these have long been taken as evidence of the deterioration of control over the bureaucracy created by the decades of disorder. But this material does not, in fact, differ very much from the attempts to control the administrators which are attested as early as the third century B.C., and, had we not an awareness of the domestic turmoil, we would have no difficulty in fitting *P. Tebt.* 5 into the long history of efforts on the part of Alexandria to regulate the activities of officials in the *chora*.

I am not trying to assert that the dynastic troubles of the second century had nothing to do with weakening the dynasty, or that there was no change in administrative patterns from the middle of the third to the end of the second centuries B.C. Rather, I am trying to suggest that the developments may have been more independent of one another, with administrative changes proceeding from their own internal logic, facilitated, perhaps, but not caused by the difficulties of the kings and queens, and that even without the dynastic troubles these changes would have occurred, although perhaps a little more slowly. In the same way, the damage done to the countryside by the dynastic wars probably did not act very strongly as a cause of weakness at the center. It is important to remember that, for all the commercial activity like the lending of money, mortgaging of property, sale of goods, inheritances and divisions thereof, marriages and manipulations of dowries, transport and shipping which we have attested in our papyri and which focused the attention of scholars on the trading aspects of Ptolemaic society, the economy always remained fundamentally agricultural. It was also an agricultural economy that generated wealth almost exclusively from what farmers today call "cash crops," that is, sown, reaped and sold within one agricultural year. Because of the nature of Egyptian agriculture, furthermore, prosperity was influenced almost entirely by the rise of the Nile, and even in times of turmoil little long-term damage could be done by troops or fighting. The amount of loss which might obtain from losses of orchards and vineyards was a very small part of the agricultural bounty of the land, and the potential of loss in fertilization from destruction of animals had relatively little impact on the soil.

At the same time, the fundamentally non-coinage orientation of the vast majority of peasant activity in Egypt made coin-oriented segments of the administration of lesser importance in the aggregate of official activity, and significant rather to that very small body of Greek-speaking members of the population who actually had to do with commerce. It was this group who would feel any effects of the copper inflation of the end of the third century,[26] and it was the need for coin, copper as well as silver—progressively in short supply—by members of this group that made positions in the paid administration attractive. Furthermore, the labor excess of Egypt, which I believe obtained even in antiquity,[27] meant that for the small number of Greeks and Macedonians in Egypt, there was an adequate supply of natives to work the land profitably as rentees or sharecroppers, so that salaried positions with the king, and any commercial transactions which might be possible, became attractive as offering opportunities of money-making. That the administrative positions were seen as desirable is clear from the fact that money was paid to obtain them. And certainly the attempts of *P Tebt.* 5 to prohibit abuses at the end of the second century B.C. shows that the officials were still finding means of taking advantage of their positions.

These considerations should warn us against the assumption of a link between political disruption and economic decline. There is certainly evidence that, despite the troubles of the second century, and even later, down into the first, Egypt was still able

---

[26]Tony Reekmans, "Economic and Social Repercussions of the Ptolemaic Copper Inflation," *Chronique d'Égypte* 48 (1949), pp. 324-342; "The Ptolemaic Copper Inflation," *Ptolemaica* (Studia Hellenistica 7, Lovanii, 1951), pp. 61-118.

[27]I should point out that this view is not the conventional one of labor shortage, expressed by Rostovtzeff, *SEHHW* I, p. 287, but is based on an understanding of the excess manpower available in modern Egypt in a situtation which saw a good proportion of the land, as in antiquity, devoted to cereal crops: G.S. Saab, *The Egyptian Agrarian Reform* (Oxford, 1967). For the full argument, see my "Money Economy," *BASP* 21 (1984), p. 197.

to afford its king vast wealth, and it is only Auletes who was credited with dissipating it. And even this, we should note, was done not by disruption of the economy or the administrative structure, but by the king's lavish foreign expenditure in quest of his own re-establishment in Alexandria. The administrative structure remained intact, a body of practice and officials which existed to be reformed and controlled only by the force of the Roman takeover, and even the wealth of the country had the potential, despite Auletes' profligacy, to make Cleopatra VII an invaluable ally to Antony and a genuine threat to Octavian's secure tenure of Rome and Italy.

A re-evaluation of the relationship between the crown and the bureaucracy makes it possible to understand how it was possible for the economy and the administration to survive so well after so long a period of weak or non-existent central government. We must, in fact, re-examine the bureaucracy at all levels to challenge the standing assumption that its structure was designed and implemented as a coherent plan on the part of Ptolemy Soter or Philadelphus, and that changes, like the increase in authority for the *strategos* or the implementation of the honorary court ranks in the early second century, owed their inception to deliberate plans or goals of the king or his highest officials in Alexandria. We can probably understand the history of Ptolemaic Egypt much better when we recognize that the bureaucracy had a vigorous life of its own, that it developed, changed and operated in response to its internal logic rather than as an agent of Alexandrian authority, and that the success and long life of the dynasty owed something to the independence of the administration. We also, then, can more easily understand how the kings carried on both foreign and internal conflict. The exploitation of Egypt, a phenomenon emphasized by Turner, was certainly in evidence, but excessive exploitation was not a feature of royal intention but rather was the effect of the administrative self-interest of the structure which emerged in the third century. The direct control of the country by Alexandria, achieved and maintained for the most part by brute force and imposed by the use of an army, meant that the administrative structure was forced to yield, overall, a good deal of the agricultural surplus, but that administrative structure was never very answerable, at least at middle and lower levels, to the will of Alexandria. The kings' repeated efforts to assert such control, in evidence for the most part in *ad hoc* situations, illustrates this characteristic of the government. It was a government in which, expressed most simply, the control of Egypt as a whole rested in Alexandria, but administration was vested in the bureaucracy.

V

THE IDEOLOGY OF PTOLEMAIC MONARCHY

If there is validity in my argument that the administration of Egypt did not emerge exclusively from the plans or objectives of Philadelphus or his successors in the dynasty, then our current conception of royal ideology in Ptolemaic Egypt changes to some extent. As I observed in connection with the discussion of the nature of monarchy under the immediate successors, the adjustment to administration which faced Alexander's generals seems not to have been met to any great extent, even by Ptolemy I Soter, and I concluded that the development of the bureaucratic structure belonged to the period of the next generation. In Egypt, it is clear that the highly articulated bureaucracy which we associate with the Ptolemaic regime was in place by the middle of the third century B.C., and that quite a large number of Greek-speaking and Greek-writing officials were carrying on duties based on accumulation of rules and experience which went back at least a few decades. The existence of regulations issued in the name of the king, some dated by years earlier than those for which we have the bulk of our evidence, shows that the beginnings of the development of the system can be traced back at least to the early years of Philadelphus. It could hardly be argued for a king like Philadelphus that this evidence for royal direction could be attributed to a chancery operating independently of a king, such as we might find during the minority rule of such Ptolemies as Epiphanes and Philometor. Yet even with an active king, intervening in or at least issuing orders to the administration, the ideology of kingship at the time of Philadelphus must have been very different from that which we would imagine from a concept which saw him remaking, if not originating, the extensive administrative structure, and reorganizing the economy of Egypt along rational and purposeful lines.

If we are to seek an ideology of Philadelphus' kingship, we could ask for nothing more explicit than Theocritus XVIIth idyll. In a eulogy to Philadelphus in traditional Hellenic mode, the praises of the king follow Greek patterns of ideas in a form which is essentially that of Homeric hymn. The virtues for which Theocritus praises Ptolemy are themselves Homeric and

Pindaric—fighting prowess, munificence, wealth, genesis from divinity. Nothing in Theocritus' language suggests that Ptolemy II was different in quality from the kings and aristocrats of early Greece. Theocritus also praises Philadelphus' great father, Ptolemy, associating him with divinity through descent from Heracles and by proximity to Alexander. Himself a god, the great conqueror and his relationship to Ptolemy appear in terms evocative of Zeus seated on Olympus. Philadelphus' mother, Berenice, duly receives praise, and Theocritus claims apotheosis for her, that she never went down in death to Acheron, but Aphrodite "snatched her before she encountered the dark ship and the grim ferryman of those who have come to their end, setting her up in a temple."[1] The poem is filled with allusions to Zeus; "We begin with Zeus," Theocritus opens his paean of praise, and the poem ends with the Olympian, in a traditional form of closing such a poem:

"Rejoice, lord Ptolemy. I am mindful of you, equal of the other demigods, and I believe I speak a word which will not fail to reach those to come in the future. And for virtue, from Zeus pray."

The poem, so evocative of early Greek poetry, applies the themes of earliest Greek tradition, themes established for the city-states of the fifth century B.C. and in place long before the conquests of Alexander and the wars of the successors, and it is not unique. The remnants of Callimachus' *Lock of Berenice* present at length the same concept of the apotheosis of Berenice as Theocritus' short passage.[2] This ideology of monarchy assembles many of the ideas with which we are familiar from Alexander's pattern of kingship: divine ancestry, ability in war, reverence toward the gods and display and generous use of great wealth. The Alexander-tradition stressed Alexander's demonstration of these traits in its coherent view of the conqueror, and Theocritus applies them to Ptolemy as well. While these qualities by no means exhaust those which might have been expected of a monarch, they certainly would have been prominent among those regarded as flattering to the king, and they are royal characteristics central to any concept of the nature of a king.

[1]Theoc. XVII, 48-49.
[2]*Aitia* 110; Catullus 66.

THE IDEOLOGY OF PTOLEMAIC MONARCHY

Certainly, the attitudes toward kingship held by Ptolemy I would be important in developing the ideology of the Ptolemaic monarchy, and the stories about Alexander attributed to Ptolemy with the consistently favorable slant they take may go back to the king's own history of the great conqueror. If this were the case, we would have in Ptolemy's version of Alexander a kingship of character and personality, not a kingship of government and accomplishment, a kingship closer to Theocritus' Philadelphus than to the royal bureaucrat of modern scholarship.

We have too often tended to separate the conceptions of Theocritus from an assumed reality of government and power operated by Philadelphus. The poet praises as a traditional bard, so we do not take his expressions as serious notions of divinity impinging on the royal family. So too, the numerous uses of the royal oath as they appear in the papyri are not taken seriously—in religious terms—or used to determine the impact the notion of royal divinity might have had on Greeks in Egypt, even though the king's significance in the oath parallels that of the gods in usage.[3] There is no doubt that this formal acceptance of a divine quality inhering in the king is a feature of kingship which emerged out of the traditions surrounding Alexander the Great, and that concept, for the Macedonians at least, was grounded in attitudes which had permitted Philip to present himself as a thirteenth of the gods at the marriage of his daughter Cleopatra in 336. There was a ready acceptance of the application of the idea to Soter and the Ptolemies among the Greek cities in the establishment of royal cults in many centers,[4] and the Ptolemaic dynasty itself carried the concept to a new and more complex structure.

Philadelphus—if not Soter—took the ideas of divinity which had been bruited as early as the cult honors to Ptolemy I by the Rhodians and on Delos and formalized them in the dynastic cult. That cult now no longer depended on the gratitude of cities

---

[3]See my comments in "The Ptolemies and the Ideology of Kingship," delivered at the Symposium on Hellenistic History and Culture, at the University of Texas at Austin, in October, 1988.

[4]The best treatment of the royal—as against dynastic—cults in the Greek states, with the Macedonian precedents remains that of Christian Habicht, *Gottmenschentum und Griechische Städte* (Zetemata 14, Munich, 1956, 2nd ed. 1970).

THE IDEOLOGY OF PTOLEMAIC MONARCHY

or the whims of politics, in the manner of the royal cults of the Greek cities elsewhere, but rather became a statement by the king-god himself and established the concept of the monarch as god for Greeks and Macedonians who then could serve him in patterns familiar to them. The dynastic cult itself has long been seen as an aspect of the ideology of Ptolemaic monarchy, but it has not been studied much as an institution. Surveys like those of Cerfaux and Taeger[5] have sought to place the Ptolemaic cult in its place as part of a long development before and after the third century, and so presented what is more or less a summary of the formal developments in the cult. Even the recent surveys by Préaux and the *Cambridge Ancient History* have done little more than describe the evolution of the cult as it was expanded to include Philadelphus and Arsinoe, the *Theoi Adelphoi*, the *Theoi Euergetai* in the generation after that, and then reorganized to put the cult of the *Theoi Soteres* in with the others, in their proper sequence from Alexander on.

A full study of the cult, its cult places and its priests would be rewarding; a great deal more is known about all of these since Otto wrote,[6] and the examination of the eponymous priests by Ijsewijn produced the conclusion that they came from the court circle,[7] a view widely accepted and repeated in Fraser's discussion.[8] But we lack an analysis of documents with and without priestly dating formulae to determine if there exists any pattern which might throw light on the role the cult played in the society, and we may also be able to learn something from a careful review of any activities devoted to the cult. It would only be such detailed studies that would permit us to judge whether there is any validity in Taeger's denigration of the religious character of the cult, claiming, on the basis of some of Philadelphus' arrangements, the "fragwürdigen religiösen Charakter des

---

[5]L. Cerfaux, J. Tondriau, *Le Culte des souverains dans la civilization gréco-romaine: un concurrent du christianisme* (Bibliothèque de Théologie, Ser. 3, 5, Tournai, 19560; F. Taeger, *Charisma: Studien zur Geschichte des antiken Herrscherkultes* (Stuttgart, 1956).

[6]W. Otto, *Priester und Tempel in Hellenistischen Ägypten* (Leipzig-Berlin, 1905, 1908).

[7]J. Ijsewijn, *De Sacerdotibus Sacerdotiisque Alexandri Magni et Lagidarum Eponymis* (Brussels, 1961); new lists now available in W. Clarysse and G. van der Weken, *The Eponymous Priests of Ptolemaic Egypt* (Leiden, P. Lugduno-Batava 24, 1983).

[8]P.M. Fraser, *Ptolemaic Alexandria* I, p. 223.

dynastischen Kultes,"[9] or whether we might move beyond Fraser's assessment that the cult "nevertheless cannot be dismissed as a fiction designed purely to give prestige to holders of paper priesthoods."[10] An understanding of the dynastic cult as well as the royal cult is part of the broader problem of comprehending the religious and sociological character of the spread of Egyptian cults in general in the Mediterranean world, with all the difficulties and complexities recently reviewed by Françoise Dunand, pointing out some of the new collections of evidence and possibilites of using this evidence to throw light on religious mentalities.[11] The potential religious significance of the cult is supported, it seems to me, by the other aspects and attributes of divinity which may be assembled: identification of the sovereigns with deities, and the more common assimilation of queens with female divinities such as Isis and Aphrodite, the establishment of temples to members of the dynasty, temples to them either individually or in association with other deities, dedications connected with public cults of the sovereigns discrete from the dynastic cult itself which show private dedications to them either as deities themselves or as assimilated to other deities.[12]

Perhaps even more significant are the representations of the Ptolemies, in the first two centuries of the dynasty. By this I do not mean the coin portraits, in particular the dual representations like those of Philadelphus-Arsinoe which have been interpreted to emphasize the dynastic, rather than individual, aspect of kingship. Rather more significant for private cult are the many marble heads, from the time of Philadelphus on, which were made to be affixed to figures made of less-expensive and more easily obtainable material like wood. Kyrielis very reasonably sees these figures as presented for "private people, officials, soldiers or townspeople. . .cult

---

[9]*Charisma*, p. 297.

[10]*Ptolemaic Alexandria* I, p. 225; the opinion challenged is that of Ijsewijn, *Sacerdotibus*, p. 158.

[11]F. Dunand, "Cultes égyptiens hors d'Égypte: Nouvelles voies d'approche et d'interpetation," *Egypt and the Hellenistic World*, pp. 75-98.

[12]The evidence for these aspects of divinity is reviewed by Fraser, *Ptolemaic Alexandria* I, pp. 226-246, and notes thereto.

representations, in private royal cult chapels or in local gymnasia or as dedications of loyal servants."[13] Whether these are merely expressions of loyalty or represent a genuine religious sense, the frequency of their appearance, the proliferation of royal representations in terracotta and plaster,[14] and the faience oinochoai used as ritual vessels in some way for cult purpose,[15] all demonstrate the spread of the royal cults and perhaps the dynastic cult far beyond the direct action of the crown. The significance of all this for the spiritual aspect of the ruler cult and the divine aspects of the members of the dynasty may be pointed up by the frequency of representations of female members. Assimilation of the queens to Isis must surely have had an impact on attitudes towards the living rulers on the part of Greeks; if the greater sympathy toward the spiritual value of the Isis (and Sarapis) cult on the part of some modern commentators provides a lead,[16] we might be willing to take more seriously the very plentiful evidence that the Ptolemies fitted in some genuine way into the relationship with the divine maintained by the Greeks in Egypt.

If cult and divinity were an aspect of the ideology, so too was, on the human level, military accomplishment and adventure. Soter participated fully in the military conflicts which marked the last two decades of the fourth century B.C., and despite ups and downs of defeat and victory, he could claim to have been, on balance, more successful than his peers. He preserved Egypt

[13]Helmut Kyrielis, *Bildnisse der Ptolemäer* (Ägyptische Forschungen 2, Berlin, 1975), pp. 145-146. Kyrielis, in drawing his summary conclusions about the significance of the marble and coin portraits, emphasizes the difference between the Ptolemaic iconography and that of the contemporary kings elsewhere in the third century, follows traditional views of the centralizing nature of the monarchy in seeing these figures as expressions of the loyalty of the subjects.

[14]R. A. Lunsingh Scheurleer, "Ptolemies?", *Das Ptolemäische Ägypten*, pp. 1-22. It is worth noting that Scheurleer emphasized the distinction between the portraits of Egyptian type and those "made in the Hellenistic tradition," while Kyrielis sees that his portraits do not often betray Egyptian stylization, but wants to see an Egyptian pull influencing them (p. 158).

[15]Dorothy B. Thompson, *Ptolemaic Oinochoai and Portraits in Faience: Aspects of the Ruler Cult* (Oxford, 1973).

[16]J. Gwyn Griffiths, "The Great Egyptian Cults of Oecumenical Spiritual Significance," in A.H. Armstrong, ed., *Classical Mediterranean Spirituality* (London, 1986), pp. 66-101.

always safe from rivals, from the time of Perdiccas' attack on; he was on the winning side which ended Antigonus' career at Ipsus in 301; he survived everyone but Lysimachus and Seleucus, and they died in battle or by assassination, while he left his heir secure and with an enormous war machine. Philadelphus in turn was at war or adventuring successfully at the end of the 280s, fought a war with Antiochus I in the second half of the 270s, involved himself in the Chremonidean War in the 260s and then undertook the Second Syrian War at the end of that decade and carried it on for several years.[17] The third Ptolemy began his reign with another Syrian War, one in which he was triumphant enough to justify the praises of the Canopus Decree which record his return of the Egyptian Gods from Syria. Even Philopator, who is reported as notably unambitious, could claim the success of Raphia in 217.

I am certainly not trying to claim the reputation of a great conqueror for Philopator, or even for Euergetes I, despite his success in Syria. The references to the third and fourth Ptolemies merely show their continuance, perhaps forced on them, of military activity. But for Philadelphus I think the frequent military activity down to mid-century justifies, to some extent, Theocritus' boast that Berenice produced "a spear-bearing Ptolemy for spear-bearing Ptolemy,"[18] even if he were a stay-at-home commander and suffered some notable failures, like that of the Chremonidean War.

Despite the activist military stance, by the mid 250s Philadelphus' international position had deteriorated seriously. Eric Turner insisted that the first thirty years of the reign was a period of warfare which led to a financial squeeze on Egypt,[19] and whether or not one agrees with the claim that the administration was driven centrally by the king's needs, Turner's assessment of military expense and strain is much more appropriate to the evidence of Philadelphus' activity in

---

[17]I make this point in greater detail in "The Ptolemies and the Ideology of Kingship," delivered at the Symposium on Hellenistic History and Culture, at the University of Texas at Austin, in October, 1988.

[18]Theoc. XVII, 56-57.

[19]CAH^2, VII, pp. 135-159.

those years than is the more common view of the king as a genial and pacific ruler.

There has been a great deal of discussion of the purposes of the Ptolemaic policy which, Turner claims, bankrupted Egypt. There has been debate over whether the first two kings of the dynasty fought to preserve trade advantages or were concerned primarily to preserve the cordon of overseas possessions as a protection of their hold on Egypt. Rostovzteff has argued that they were concerned only with Egypt itself, but that the need to provide the resources on which to base a fleet and army drew them into overseas adventures to obtain those resources. It will come as no surprise that I see the explanation of the "imperialism" of Philadelphus less in terms of economic or political strategy than arising out of royal self-image and expectations of a king's behavior. It seems to me that Philadelphus could not accept territorial losses or fail to exploit opportunities for acquisition and expect to maintain the respect of his forces or continue in the regard of the Greeks and Macedonians as a king in the tradition of his father, of Alexander and Philip. That tradition presented a king as fighting to maintain his *pragmata*, which included the territories over which he had control. Looking back at the notion of the well-being of the king, his friends and his *pragmata* mentioned in regard to Lysimachus, Philadelphus would naturally react to threats by fighting.

Besides the aspects of divinity and leadership in war, Theocritus emphasizes Philadelphus' wealth and munificence. Those characteristics have certainly been recognized by modern writers as well as Philadelphus' contemporaries. The creation of the scientific and cultural centers which made up the museion and library were not only parallels to Alexander's interests in and encouragement of intellectual pursuits, they represented a great outlay of money. The king built, and paid and attracted to Alexandria a clutch of the most famous—Archimedes, Callimachus, Theocritus and others—and assured himself and his court of a reputation which would last the ages. Calleixinus' report of the great procession of Philadelphus details the floats and exhibits paraded through Alexandria, a display of wealth as well as ingenuity,[20] and the huge army which followed the religious paraders supports the claims of military strength and resources we find in Theocritus and Appian.[21] In civil life and outside Alexandria, the gifts of the great *doreai*, like the 10,000-*aroura* estate of Apollonius which encompassed a whole village, and the distribution of cleruchies to the Greeks and Macedonians in Egypt can be seen as generosity as well as economic in force, perhaps part of the gifts to his "good companions."[22] His reign also saw a burst of temple construction, not only for Greek cults but for Egyptian as well, and although modern scholars portray this as political in motive, aimed at accommodating the Greeks and conciliating the natives, Theocritus makes it another demonstration of his wealth and generosity.[23]

Rich, generous, warlike, godlike—so we might describe Ptolemy or Alexander. And like Philip and Alexander, Philadelphus had his "friends." Ptolemy, like other successors, had his circle of advisers and aides, Greeks and Macedonians who carried the title of "Friend" and served in high administrative, military and diplomatic capacity. The members of the royal group turn up in inscriptions in the Aegean area in the reign of the first Ptolemy and in Philadelphus' time as well, although there are few references to these *philoi* active in lesser administrative roles in the chora. The *philoi*, as well as the less-attested Bodyguards and Chief Bodyguards whose dignities seem to have lapsed by the end of the third century B.C., were clearly functionaries in Alexandria, part of the immediate circle of the king. Studies of royal activities in the Greek world make it clear that the king's agents came from this group, and his interests were carried on by it, and that his circle never grew into a formal bureaucracy in the way that the administrative structure of the chora developed.[24] So long as the kings had interests in the

---

[20]Recorded by Athenaeus, *Deipnosophistae* V, 196-203.

[21]Theoc. XVII, 90-94; Appian, *Roman History* I.5 (21-22).

[22]Theoc. XVII, 111.

[23]XVII, 106-108.

[24]R.S. Bagnall, *The Administration of the Ptolemaic Posessions Outside Egypt* (Leiden, 1976), and G. Herman, "The 'Friends' of the Early Hellenistic Rulers: Servants or Officials?" *Talanta* 12-13 (1980-1981), pp. 103-149. Herman argues that in the early period, the vagueness of titling of the officials honored by the Greek cities demonstrates the negative attitude towards court titles among the Greeks of the

THE IDEOLOGY OF PTOLEMAIC MONARCHY

Aegean or in the Mediterranean outside Alexandria—that is, through the third century B.C., the king carried on his activities through court officials of Alexandria who were not tied into the regular bureaucracy.[25] It is only after the contraction of administration into Alexandria itself that the informal government of the court circle declined in importance, and opened the way for the establishment of a purely honorific court titulature tied to the administrative machinery of the chora.[26] But until this happened, the king's government was not so different from that of Philip and Alexander's, a government by men who had direct relations with the king and titles like "friend" and "bodyguard" which emphasized this closeness.

The ideology which all these characteristics of kingship suggest is one of personal monarchy, as many have observed. As a personal monarchy, the crown itself did not elaborate its connections with the bureaucracy during the third century, and the relationship between king and population was conceived as a direct connection, rather than one proceeding through the layers of administration. We can see this particularly clearly in the formulae of petitions. Although a reasonably articulated judicial structure was in place by mid-century, the petitions represented by the *Enteuxeis* collection and others among Hibeh texts and papyri from other parts of Egypt strongly indicate a sense that the king was, for the Greeks at least, the source of justice and was to be approached directly. From the last years of Euergetes I and the beginning of the reign of Philopator—before the advent of the ruling ministers—the petitions are addressed

time; the assembly of texts identifying the Ptolemaic officers who are honored further shows that for the most part, and except for military ranks, their importance in the Ptolemaic context appears in their court titles rather than bureaucratic or administrative ranks.

[25]Fraser, *Ptolemaic Alexandria* I (Oxford, 1972), pp. 101-105, distinguishes for the third century "dual administrative spheres;" one operating outside Egypt and using the personal representatives of the king, who were, for the most part, Greeks, Alexandrians and Macedonians, and another dealing with the chora in Egypt itself, which he thought was staffed for the most part by lower-class Alexandrian citizens and non-privileged Greeks of Alexandria.

[26]For this, see Leon Mooren, *The Aulic Titulature in Ptolemaic Egypt, Introduction and Prosopography* (Brussels, 1975) and "The Ptolemaic Court System," *Chronique d'Égypte* 60 (1985) 214-222.

directly to the king, they complain that the petitioner has personally suffered the described wrong, and they ask that the king intervene directly by instructing the strategus to take the desired action.

I am not interested here in the question of the evolution of the importance of the strategus in the bureaucratic system, but rather in the fact that the petitions represented by these texts do not transcend his office and proceed to the king as they are addressed. The strategus acts on the petitions himself. In general, what is asked by the complainant, after explaining the wrong suffered, is that the king order the strategus to write to a subordinate official to act on the matter in one way or another—investigating, sending the accused for questioning, or follow some such procedure. What our papyri show is that the strategus' office takes the requested step by subscribing that instruction to the petition itself, and that there is no paper trail indicating that the papyrus ever proceeded to the king. Indeed, as *P.Enteuxis* 22 demonstrates, where there is a paper trail, it shows that the document was handed in to the strategus' office in the nome, rather than being sent to Alexandria.

Although there are complaints to all sorts of officials in the bureaucracy attested by our texts, and the *enteuxeis* themselves refer to the possibility of "settling the disputants" by members of the administration or the courts, the *enteuxis* petitions retain and show the sense of the king as the object of appeal for justice. And the appeal is direct, on a bi-lateral basis. There is no procedure attested whereby officials are requested to transmit petitions or complaints to the king, nor are there papyri which ask for access to the king. The few texts which ask an official or personage at court to use influence with the king all emanate from personal connections and not from procedural structure. What the petitions illustrate, I think, is a sense that although a bureaucracy exists and does most of the work, it does not block the direct link between the king and the individual. The officials act, but the king moves the administration, perhaps almost like an abstract force, and like a god, the king may be approached directly to do that.

The ideology of the monarchy as it developed among the Greeks in Egypt in the third century B.C. left the king his traditional quality of military leader, and reinforced the sense of

THE IDEOLOGY OF PTOLEMAIC MONARCHY

kingship as endowing or comprehending divinity. It also contained a sense of the king as a leader of a group of companions, the *hetaroi* of Alexander, the *philoi* or "friends" of the king, who along with Greeks noted for literary and scientific accomplishments came to Egypt during the reigns of Ptolemy I and II to make Alexandria a literary and scientific center of pan-Mediterranean class. But the Ptolemies never solved the problem of incorporating administration into the concept of monarchy, of fitting , somehow, the idea of the divine adventurer and his friends into a hierarchical structure whereby the royal power flowed downward through the various ranks of officials and endowed them with the authority to govern the land. At the end of the third century, at least, the relationship between king and subject was still direct, notionally, and that idea of the bilateral relationship between king and individual influenced the development of the Ptolemaic monarchy, as we can see from the documents which emerged from the confusing decades of the second century.

The *philanthropa* issued by the kings in the second century B.C., and in particular the long and seemingly comprehensive text of *P.Tebt.* 5 have generally been understood to reflect attempts at the reorganization of administration after a long period of dynastic conflict among Euergetes II, his brother and his sister. The text is a typical, if full, example of the *philanthropa* issued by the Ptolemies, texts which illustrate the ideology which makes the king the personal protector of the people. This notion inheres in the direct relationship exemplified by the petitions of the end of the third century, and it is part of the ideology of kingship which is taken to have been developed by philosophers and propagandists of the second century, and it is in that century that we see these concepts reflected in official texts. Whereas the cautions against abuses in the third-century *P.Tebt.* 703 are related directly to protection of the revenues, the remissions in *P.Tebt.* 5 are stated as good-will grants; it is modern analysts who relate them to a desire to reconstruct the taxation base. In fact, the document and its provisions are, I think, as much intended as *philanthropa* emanating from the ideology of kingship as they are reflective of unrest in Egypt. These amnesties, first issued in the second century B.C., became a feature of later Ptolemaic history, and may be genuine attempts to settle unrest and signify

78

better times coming, as is generally said. They also attest a development in the ideology of kingship, an ideology which, as Schubart pointed out a long time ago,[27] emphasized the king's role as a helper and exemplar of moral ideals. There are, after all, alternatives to *philanthropa* in dealing with unrest and unruly subjects; Antiochus IV tried one in Palestine in the same general period when we first find the *philanthropa* appearing in Egypt. Antiochus did not succeed in his attempt to assert control through force and assault on the Jews of Palestine, but his failure was a failure in a different place and under different circumstances than those of Egypt, and it was an approach which the Ptolemies might have used. That they did not has as much or more to do with ideology, the concept of kingship which had developed by that time in Egypt, which, I suggest, determined the manner in which Philometor and Euergetes II would respond to the problems of asserting themselves as kings.

The Egyptian materials are helpful in understanding the monarchy as it appeared to the natives. Whatever might be the extent of the desire of Euergetes II later to "conciliate" the native priesthood, texts like those carved between 144/3 and 142 on the Egyptian temple of Tôd show the impact of dynastic turmoil on iconography. The king and queen (Euergetes II and Cleopatra II) along with their predecessors, are given a prominence which suggests a recognition of equality for Cleopatra II.[28] The insistence on dynastic continuity represented would fit into a conceptualization of "good" kings who have long reigns and are succeeded by their sons, or "bad," who experience the converse, an ideology which appears in the Demotic Chronicle, and which applies to the Ptolemies as well as "native" rulers.[29]

---

[27]Wilhelm Schubart, "Das hellenistische Königsideal nach Inschriften und Papyri," *Archiv für Papyrusforschung* 12 (1937), pp. 1-26.

[28]As argued by J.-C. Grenier, "Ptolémée Evergète II et Cléopâtre II d'après les textes du temple de Tôd," *Alessandria e il mondo ellenistico-romano, Studi in onore di Achille Adriani* I (Rome 1983), pp. 32-37, in this short period before Euergetes II expelled his sister from power and married Cleopatra III, an effort was being made to impress reconciliation on any who would comprehend the representation on the temple.

[29]As definition of legitimate kingship, based on earlier Egyptian concepts of kingship: J. Johnson, "The Demotic Chronicle as a Statement of a Theory of Kingship," *Journal of the Society for the Study of Egyptian Antiquities* 13, 61-72.

THE IDEOLOGY OF PTOLEMAIC MONARCHY

Dynastic conflict began again after the death of Ptolemy VIII, among his heirs, his wife Cleopatra III and his two sons, Soter II and Alexander, and in the first year, with Cleopatra III involved as well. Cleopatra III dominated the scene at first, with Soter II ruling as Ptolemy IX, with the reign interrupted briefly in 110-109, again in the year after, and in 107 by Alexander for a long period down to 88, when Alexander died; Soter II then returned and ruled until his death in 80; that was a year of confusion in which first Cleopatra Berenice governed for six months, then Alexander II, Ptolemy XI, until he was slaughtered by the enraged Alexandrians for killing Berenice 19 days after his association with her on the throne. That leaving the throne empty with no legitimate successor, the Alexandrians chose a so-called "bastard" son of Soter II to rule as Ptolemy XII, and this king ruled, with interruptions, until 51. He was entirely dependent on Roman support to maintain himself on the throne; between 58 and 55 he was in Rome, bribing and petitioning to have himself recognized as king and, achieving that, installed again in Alexandria in 55. The last Ptolemies, Cleopatra VII and Ptolemy XIII were associated on the throne with Auletes in 52, ruled independently after his death in 51, disputed with one another until first Ptolemy XIII was eliminated in 47, then Ptolemy XIV in 44, leaving Cleopatra to bring the dynasty to a close in the last paroxysms of the Roman civil wars.

After the reign of Ptolemy IX Soter II there is little evidence of the Ptolemaic rulers acting in ways that suited the abstract concepts of kingship I have elucidated here. The derogatory remarks of Polybius about the Alexandrians and his descriptions of the kings suggest quite strongly that by mid-second century, the rulers in Alexandria were seen as voluptuaries and failures as rulers. Even so, some of the basic qualities of kingship which are apparent in the ideology as it emerged in the third century B.C. persisted right to the end of the dynasty, the dynastic cult and ruler cults still strong enough to be adapted to Roman successors,[30] the circle of "friends" still around the king, Alexandria still a cultural center with literary and philosophical

---

[30]Even if a good deal of the evidence comes from demotic rather than Greek texts of this period.

earlier expression of the ruler's concern for the people, with grants of asylum, benefits to temples and priests. A text of Auletes' reign[31] granting privileges to cleruchs and amnesty for crimes presents the same kind of administrative clemency as had the decree of Euergetes II in the previous century, and the so-called "last decree of the Ptolemies," an order of Cleopatra VII of 41 B.C., gives the traditional image of the monarch as protecting the people against the bureaucracy, the monarch "greatly hating the wicked and adjudging a common and universal vengeance" in forbidding officials from exacting of excessive payments.[32]

There is a coherence and a consistency in the manner in which the members of the Ptolemaic dynasty present themselves to us in their official acts, in their decrees, their inscriptions, the honors they give and receive, for most of the kings and for most of the period in which they reigned. The coherence reflects an ideology which served both the kings and populace, and it is an ideology which was explicitly expressed for all by the words of Theocritus almost as the concepts were forming. These were rulers who were great because they were wealthy, because they were generous, faithful to the gods, warriors—great warriors—at least as the dynasty began, and all this, no doubt, due in part to their nature as divinities themselves. These were ideas of kingship which can be traced back to earlier concepts in Greek tradition, and they were concepts which would re-emerge as part of monarchic ideology later. But the ideology did not include an idea of ordered government, of administration, of attention to and regulation of detail, of the monarch as the directing head of a complex bureaucracy. For that addition to the ideology of royalty, Egypt would wait for the Romans.

[31] *BGU* 1185 of 60 B.C. = *C.Ord.Ptol.* 71.
[32] *C.Ord.Ptol.* 76.22-23.

VI

PTOLEMAIC EGYPT AND HISTORICAL INTERPRETATION

Ptolemaic Egypt, which long served historians as an example of the spread of Hellenism to the "barbarian" east and of the adaptation of Greeks to eastern culture, has more and more come to represent qualities of cultural chauvinism among the Greeks. The period of Greek and Macedonian control in Egypt thus becomes a continuation of Hellenic patterns, rather than a radical break with the past. The "interpretatio Graeca" of non-Greek religion by Herodotus and others, the near-unanimous rejection of the learning of foreign languages by Greeks, the disdain for barbarians clear in the writings of Aristotle, these and so many features of Greek cultural values earlier were not overturned by the migration of Greeks eastwards.

Perceptions that Greeks and Macedonians in Egypt held on to their customary attitudes and practices in detail and in essence has meant that historians of antiquity no longer can find that the three centuries of Ptolemaic rule in Egypt "prepared" the way for religious, social, political and cultural features which they find in Roman times. Insofar as fundamental changes overtook the Greek world with the advent of the Roman world state and later the growth of Christianity, those changes now should be interpreted more in terms of the characteristics of Roman society and government, and of Christianity in the hellenized form in which it was carried to the Greek East and Latin West. Challenges like that of Naphtali Lewis to the very concept of "Greco-Roman Egypt"[1] show that the idea of unity and continuation from Ptolemaic times to Roman in Egypt is dissolving, and the sense of a gulf between the two eras emerges the more forcefully from the revision of the old notions of cultural development in Egypt after the conquest by Alexander.

In a similar way, we can no longer use Ptolemaic Egypt as a stage in the development of the administrative monarchy characteristic of Roman government. Many historians no longer

---

[1]"'Greco-Roman Egypt': Fact or Fiction?" *Proceedings of the Twelfth International Congress of Papyrology* (American Studies in Papyrology 7, Toronto, 1970), pp. 3-14.

see the Ptolemaic administrative structure as a salutary rationalization of a near eastern bureaucracy, using the progressive forces of Hellenism to create a new form of monarchy responsible for a substantial advance in material civilization. Insofar as there was an advance in material well-being, it will be seen to owe its impetus to other, perhaps impersonal forces, and the Ptolemaic monarchy seems to some, at least, to have been a negative influence. The Macedonian administration itself can no longer be presented confidently as a planned, reasoned application of government to the agricultural and economic problems of Egypt. More and more we are seeking to find parallels for Ptolemaic institutions in the scanty earlier Egyptian sources. The evidence on the Greek side suggests that the administration of Egypt on the part of the monarchy was less planned, less coherent and less successful than has hitherto been alleged. On reflection, that should come as no surprise. Public administration in the Greek world was notably exiguous, Macedonian bureaucracy down to the reign of Philip II was practically non-existent, and the structures established by Alexander the Great were, in general, those he found in place, and they were staffed by natives supervised in a military way by Macedonians and Greeks left as guards and garrisons.

In the long run, the utility of these new perceptions and suggestions will depend on whether the conclusions of recent scholarship are supported by new evidence and convincing new interpretations. In any case, whether or not the Hegelian concept of advance through thesis and antithesis proves valid for Ptolemaic Egypt, it is clear that our concept of Ptolemaic Egypt has moved past the initial thesis of "fusion" engendered by the first century of study of the materials of Hellenic Egypt in the centuries after Alexander.

Alan E. Samuel is Professor of Greek and Roman History at the University of Toronto. He has held a Guggenheim Fellowship and research fellowships from the Social Sciences and Humanities Research Councils of Canada. He was a founding member of The American Society of Papyrologists which he has served both as Secretary-Treasurer and President. He was the first editor of *The Bulletin of the American Society of Papyrology* and the monograph series *American Studies in Papyrology*.

Samuel's publications in Greek and Roman history include: *Ptolemaic Chronology*, *Greek and Roman Chronology* (in the *Handbuch der Altertumswissenschaft*), *Myceneans in History*, *Yale Papyri in the Beinecke Rare Book and Manuscript Library* I, *Death And Taxes: Ostraka in the Royal Ontario Museum* I, and *From Athens to Alexandria: Hellenism and Social Goals in Ptolemaic Egypt.* His most recent book, *The Promise of the West: The Greek World, Rome and Judaism,* is a broad study of the influential aspects of Hellenism from Homer to the first century.